The Marvin Kitman
TV Show

The Marvin Kitman TV Show

Encyclopedia Televisiana

by MARVIN KITMAN, edited by Carol Kitman

OUTERBRIDGE & LAZARD, INC.
New York
Distributed by E. P. Dutton & Co.

Outerbridge & Lazard, Inc.

200 West 72 Street New York 10023

This encyclopedia could never have been compiled without my wife, Carol. She read the original literature of the field—a thousand "Marvin Kitman Show" columns—and did the editing that made a single volume possible.

During the year it took to compile, I was too busy watching television, and jotting down her observations about the programs, to help the editor much. For her assistance in this project, as in all my other work, I am grateful.

Suzy Kitman and Jamie Lincoln Kitman served as technical consultants. Television is a subject they know better than any of those other subjects they teach in the schools of New Jersey.

Andrea Jordana Kitman, 8, was especially valuable, serving as a model of the average American television viewer.

I would also like to acknowledge my debt to Mike Kolatch of the *New Leader*, who first recognized that I might be a TV critic; to Dave Laventhol of *Newsday*, who gave me a grant to continue my studies in the field; to Otis Chandler of the Los Angeles Times-Mirror Company for paying for it; and to Paul De Angelis, for tearing me away from my favorite TV programs to read the book.

But First . . . A Few Words from Your Host

It's hard to agree with the theory that there is a decline in television. The medium cannot decline further.

The print medium, of course, tells us so at the start of every season. But the doubt lingers.

Some great artistic cultures before ours, including that of Renaissance Rome, didn't take their art seriously. "What did the Italians do with great paintings?" asked Professor Reuel N. Denney in a symposium on "The Future of the Book" at the University of Chicago in 1955. "They painted them over when they got tired of them." What did they do at the first performances of great operas? "They listened," Professor Denney explained, "when they were not gossiping in the boxes."

Every time I convince myself that something like "The Jerry Lewis Show" was pure drivel, I read an item in the papers explaining that Lewis is considered a serious genius in France and Germany.

With Russ Meyer films being hailed as examples of great cinema at American college festivals, you really have to be dogmatic to believe that TV is junk. It may take 100 years or so, but the 21st century critics may discover that "Owen Marshall: Counselor at Law," "Cade's County," or even "Shirley's World" were masterpieces of 20th Century television art.

Another thing that all the critics in the TV audience keep complaining about is the lack of originality in the medium. My research shows that TV has stolen all its basic formats from radio, theater, movies, records, vaudeville and newspapers.

This may seem immoral, but there is no law against stealing ideas. The practice goes on regularly in even the more respected arts. In Emerson *vs.* Davies in 1845, the Supreme Court held: "In truth, in literature, in science, and in art, there are and can be, few, if any, things which, in an abstract sense are strictly new and original throughout . . . Virgil borrowed much from Homer; Bacon drew from earlier as well as contemporary minds; Coke exhausted all the known learning from his profession; and even Shakespeare and Milton . . . would be found to have gathered much from the abundant store of current knowledge in classical studies of their day."

While the print medium is busy criticizing the lack of creative thinking in our most (chronologically) immature art form, they ought to think back to what they were doing with their new technology in its early days. The amazing thing about the print medium is that it wasn't until seventy-five years after the invention of the printing press that anybody thought of a basic thing like numbering the pages of a book.

And why, when printing was first invented did nobody think of sitting down and writing a novel? It took two hundred years for Richardson, a printer himself, to think of that obvious way to make the medium more entertaining. Most of the books printed until then were in the news and documentaries field, i.e., Bibles and religious tracts.

Comparing the two media is not as farfetched as it may seem. The very first authenticated example of print, according to Professor Neil Postman of New York University, was an appeal asking the princes to support the Pope financially—the

2

world's first commercial. It was also the first example of advertising not working. None of the princes of that day could read.

The printing press was also the object of much hostility in its early days. People who had expensive libraries of handwritten manuscripts said the new medium printed a lot of junk. Those whose livelihood depended on manuscripts, the handletterers, also knocked it.

But the opposition to the printing press was nothing compared to what the eggheads of a still earlier day said about the written word itself. Socrates, one of the intellectual leaders during the oral period, said writing would lead to forgetfulness and rot people's minds. No wonder they got rid of him.

For the first three hundred years or so of print, people were happy just to be able to look at movable type, and I dare say it will take that long for television viewers to grow tired of the thrill of seeing pictures that move. Giving the creative geniuses at the networks the benefit of the doubt, the worst you can say about them is that after only thirty-two years of TV they may not know what else can be done with the medium.

While some of the television industry's heroic experiments are often reminiscent of man's early attempts to fly, nothing is to be gained by complaining.

A & B Sides. Making the most out of failure has been financially rewarding for the television industry. Its programs are like the "B" side of a hit record. If a record sells a million copies because of the "A" side, the "B" side shares in the royalties. In the case of television, the medium itself is the "A" side. As long as the programs move, the people buy it.

Acquisitions. Every year a handful of writers break into television. A case history of one of the lucky few, it occurred to me, might say something about the medium. Harold Robbins, the beginner picked to be studied, had his first series, "The Survivors," starring Lana Turner and George Hamilton presented by ABC from September, 1969, to January, 1970.

"Are you worried about compromising your integrity by

5

working for television?" I asked the author of *The Carpet-baggers, 79 Park Avenue,* and *The Adventurers.*

"I know it must sound that way to those familiar with my work," Robbins said. "For my next movie, *The Inheritors,* I have a deal that guarantees me three and three-quarters."

"Three and three-quarters what?" I interrupted.

"Million," Robbins explained. "I can stay on the air for three years and not get that much."

I asked him how he had gotten into this fiscal mess. "I had lunch a couple of years ago with Leonard Goldenson, the president of ABC," Robbins recalled. "I gave him a one-line synopsis of my idea: How about a TV series called 'The Survivors'?"

Robbins has always been something of a hero to many writers. What we admire most about him is his sales. The same thing can be said for Admiral Farragut. Robbins also is one of the few writers who sells his books to publishers for more than a million dollars on the basis of one-page outlines. Still, I couldn't believe that hardnosed network executives would commit themselves to a costly series by a writer without a track record, with only a sketchy story line. I was right.

"A year later," Robbins confessed, "there was a meeting about the show at ABC headquarters in New York. 'What's it going to be?' the executives asked me point blank. 'We have to know what the story is about.'

"I was curious myself. I hadn't thought it through yet. Everybody had their eyes on me as I walked over to the glass window behind Goldenson's desk. From the thirty-fifth floor—check the floor—I could see Central Park and all the way to the West 79th Street Boat Basin. There was a yacht moored in the Hudson River. I started talking the story.

" 'Here's your opening scene. The cameras focus on a yacht tied up off Manhattan. Then we zoom to a bed in a stateroom. It's a big bed. In a big stateroom. The bed has black silk sheets. In the bed, there's a blonde. She's a gorgeous blonde. She's naked—.' "

6

" 'Stop!' " Robbins recalls the executives cried, " 'We'll buy it!' "

"And then what happened?" I asked excitedly. What a relief not to be hearing another one of those dreary Merle Miller tragedies about the Hamlet-like indecisiveness of network executives.

"I went back to France and forgot about it."

At his villa in Le Cannet, Robbins resumed the life of a struggling novelist. He had finished his fourteenth novel, *The Adventurers,* and was having some writing problems with his fifteenth, *The Inheritors.* As an escape, he spent the summer working on the screenplay for *The Adventurers.*

"I slaved on that script," he explained. "I worked two hours in the morning and three hours in the afternoon on it for two months." But it all turned to ashes when the film's director didn't like the script. All Robbins got out of that distasteful experience was $250,000.

Was that what made him change his mind about risking his reputation by working for TV?

"No," Robbins said. "What happened was that Paul Gitlin, my lawyer, called me up in France and told me, 'ABC bought your idea.' "

The fifty-three-year-old balding novice TV writer said his first words upon hearing the good news were: "What idea?"

Gitlin, the lawyer who runs Robbins' creative life, said there was nothing unusual about his client's not having worked out all the details of the plot. "We structure the deal first, and then Harold worries about the writing."

Al's Father. You may have heard my friend Al's father on television last week. His laughter has been heard a thousand times since it was recorded at a Los Angeles studio. Some think he should get residuals. Many of the situation

comedies he laughs at, he once told his son, he wouldn't laugh at except for money. But he didn't go into the laugh-track business for the money. He only wanted to make the world happy.

Anchormen.
The anchorman is basically an animated script. He performs the same function for the TV viewer that linotype performs for the newspaper reader. The linotype machine has no control over content, no say in what goes out to the public. It puts a writer's words into print, or readable form, just as the anchorman puts the words of others into an audible form.

Little is known about the origin of the term "anchorman," except that it is an unfortunate choice of words. Anchor, according to the dictionary, means "come to a complete stop, a dead halt." Thus when a news show has two co-anchormen, or people as anchors, it is practically in the drydock. What makes the ship go, a reliably informed source explained, is the propellers. Dual-propellermen is a more optimistic thing for a TV station to call its news superstars.

What TV news really needs is not two propellermen or two anchormen, but two vice-presidents-in-charge-of-news, one of whom can be thrown overboard as soon as the ratings start to go down. That will halt the practice of judging news by ratings.

Applying the Fairness Doctrine.
By attacking "The Selling of the Pentagon," Vice President Agnew guaranteed that CBS News would win every journalism award in the nation in 1972. Surely the vice president can find something wrong with the other networks' news shows. The "fairness doctrine" demands that he throw the weight of his office against them immediately.

The networks desperately awaiting his help are NBC, ABC, and the Public Broadcasting Service. While they have been vaguely included in his broadside attacks since 1969, naming names wins prizes.

The most important criteria for the Agnew School of Criticism is that the target must be a program that most people haven't seen. Then a lot of people have the impression, based only on what the vice president has said about the show, that it is undermining the American or South Vietnamese position.

The smaller the audiences the better. The smallest audience for news and public affairs ever invented by modern man is on public television. PBS is a sitting duck for a vice president who can say whatever he likes about those eggheads without fear.

Unfortunately, the Public Broadcasting Service has shied away from controversy this year.

"Atlanta Sucks." See The First Amendment in Baseball.

The Average Man and Public TV.

The average man on the board of trustees of a typical public broadcasting station (in this case Channel 13 in New York) is John D. Rockefeller III. Although you can't make snap judgments about these things, I think you could make a case that Trustee Rockefeller has the public touch. One of his ancestors used to walk the streets of New York—when it was safe—handing out dimes to the people. No doubt he has been influenced by this example.

Trustee George T. Piercy, senior vice president at Standard Oil Company (New Jersey) also has his finger on the public's pulse. There is his firm's historic association with the guy who gave out the dimes, and secondly, there is all the contact he has with public groups driving past the Esso Refinery on the New Jersey Turnpike.

Then there are the ordinary people who serve on the board like Kenneth C. Foster, president of the Prudential Insurance Company of America, and Raymond C. Johnson, vice chairman of New York Life Insurance. Public TV is in good hands with them. And a lot of us owe a debt to Trustee Charles G. Stradella, who made a name for himself as chairman of the board of General Motors Acceptance Corporation.

It seems as if potential candidates for the board were asked the following questions: (1) Do you work in a bank or insurance company? (2) Are you a vice president or higher? (3) Do you work in Lower Manhattan? By applying these criteria, Channel 13 has got itself a twenty-seven-member board that any mutual fund or conglomerate would be proud of.

If educational television really wants to go public—as it did in name three years ago—Channel 13 has a golden opportunity to broaden its public appeal by electing a few really honest-to-goodness public types to the board. I'd like to make a couple of nominations.

Gus Cwizlicki runs a one-man plumbing business in Queens. If elected, his campaign manager promised me, Gus would use his influence to get the station to spend more time covering the industrial arts. "There's a tremendous amount of interest in do-it-yourself handicrafts, like replacing corroded sink traps, and Gus knows plenty about this."

Margaret Jones is a retired zipper-setter in the garment center. She is now serving society as a housewife in Rockville Centre. She would like to have a program on public television called "Morning Roulette" with George Raft as the MC (Master Croupier). "It will be like 'Hollywood Squares,'" her campaign manager said, "except the public will be able to place bets with OTB."

Michael Pignitano is a young accountant from Brooklyn College. His other qualification is that he is the cousin of a public

10

television producer. "If they let me on," his campaign statement reads, "I could show everybody how to fill out their income taxes like the Big Shots do." He even has a name for his show, "Make Your Bread At Home," and you can't deny a program like that would have mass public appeal.

"I'm not really pushing getting my cousin, the accountant, on the board," his campaign manager explained. "Actually, he's more interested in getting his program on commercial TV, where more people would see it."

There must be a lot of cousins and uncles around with free time who, if elected, would serve, and I think their names should be submitted. The power of this TV Guide is behind any qualified member of the public who will run.

Bacchus. Boy gets perfume. Boy gets girl. These are the facts advertising agencies work with in making commercials in the after-shave and cologne genre. It's not much to work with.

Still, memorable dramas have been written on the theme. The most popular in recent years—eighty percent of the television audience, it has been estimated, saw it nine times in December,

1969 alone—was a commercial for Bacchus. It retells the story of how ancient Troy fell, a subject that has fascinated dramatists from Shakespeare to Shaw.

The curtain rises on what appears to be a cast of thousands and one towering bottle of Bacchus on a flat-bed wagon parked outside the walled city of Troy. Unwitting townsmen drag the giant flagon through the gates into downtown Troy as Act I of the spectacular ends. A spigot at the base of the bottle is turned on in Act II, and the Trojan women fall prey to Bacchus' magic power. In scene after scene of wild abandon, the Trojan men fall prey to the Trojan women. As the curtain is rung down on the powerful sixty-second historical drama, it is night. A Roman soldier with his sword in his teeth is climbing out of the bottle.

"This is Bacchus," a narrator explains *sotto voce* with the authority of an Arthur Schlesinger, Jr., "the after-shave lotion that conquered the world. Bacchus. Created by the Romans in order to make their enemies irresistible to women. Because when a man is irresistible, he has better things to do with his time than fight." It was perhaps the most powerful antiwar statement ever to come out of Madison Avenue.

Some critics attack the Bacchus commercial on the ground that it may have been historically inaccurate. Well, Shakespeare and Shaw also took liberties with this period of history. I found the commercial irresistible. The other day I stopped by the offices of DKG, the New York agency that had produced the commercial for Coty, to speak with the dramatists, Neil Calet and Peter Hirsch.

It was a little disconcerting to learn that Bacchus dated back only to 1968. The scent was concocted by Coty chemists who had been ordered to find an after-shave lotion that could become an instant success in the flowering men's cosmetics market. It didn't even have a name until Calet and Hirsch thought of one.

Bacchus, it seemed to me, evokes the image of a Roman sot with grapes in his hair. Calet and Hirsch explained that Bacchus' image depends on which old painting one has seen of the Roman god. "We think of him as a teenager. Even Santa Claus is appealing as a young man."

A new after-shave lotion isn't born with a personality. The personality is acquired through the manner in which the agency says memorably: Wear this and get the girl. "The three of us thought of the metaphor of the Trojan Horse," Calet and Hirsch explained. "The first creative problem we faced was, 'Would the audience today know what the Trojan Horse was?'" Research indicated that Americans have seen enough movies on the subject to get the point.

The commercial did not use stock footage. Much to my surprise, it wasn't filmed on the outskirts of Troy, now called Ilium in Turkey. The playwrights explained that the commercial needed (1) a walled city, (2) a gate in the wall with a working door that reached eighteen feet (so a fifteen-foot bottle on a three-foot wagon could pass through) and (3) a view through the wall that didn't look like downtown Toledo. Troy failed to meet these rigorous requirements. It is in ruins. A production company was hired to find another ancient city.

Hollywood and Cinecitta in Rome had nothing to offer. For ten days the production company's talent scouts scoured France, Italy and Spain looking for the right walled city. Finally the advertising agency suggested Israel. The Lions' Gate, through which Israeli forces blasted into Old Jerusalem during the Six-Day War, became the star of the sixty-second commercial.

The cast of thousands was in fact only 175 people. Israeli students from Hebrew University in Jerusalem were signed to play warriors, townspeople and maidens. The only girl xylophonist in Israel, hired by Calet and Hirsch because she looked Swedish, plays the major supporting role of the blonde, blue-eyed girl in the window who goes crazy over the scent as it drifts up from the square. Molly Picon's niece also has a five-second scene. The real find in the cast is the Roman soldier who pops out of the bottle at the end. He is Captain Moshe Sabarav, a reserve officer in the Israeli army and a government-licensed

13

guide. "What we were looking for," Calet and Hirsch explained, "is somebody with a beard and a fierce face. The only direction we gave Sabarav was, 'Make believe it's night and you are entering a tent full of Arabs.'"

A major crisis, the producers recall, was making a proper fifteen-foot bottle. The agency felt they needed a clear green bottle. When the people in the creative department arrived on location in July, they discovered that the Israeli prop people had made an opaque bottle. They couldn't make a clear one, an unusual example of the failure of Israeli technology. A great German plastic scientist was hurriedly hired by the agency to make a clear bottle. The first one exploded. The second experimental model worked beautifully, but something in the air made it turn into a small puddle. An opaque bottle was used. "It was beautiful," Calet and Hirsch said.

One of the great commercial directors of all time, Fred Levinson (Talon zippers), was brought to Israel to film the spectacular in the manner of *El Cid* and *Ben Hur* at a rumored cost of $250,000. Calet and Hirsch say the figure is absurd: "It only cost $100,000." That's $1,666.67 a second, which could buy a lot of after-shave.

The commercial is not without redeeming social value. It undoubtedly helped the Israeli economy.

A Balanced Documentary. What a good
thing it probably is that the issue of whether the world is flat or round was decided before the invention of the TV network.

"The world is not flat," the narrator would conclude at the end of an hour-long discussion on that old argument. "We don't say it is round either," he would add. "We have just presented both sides of the controversial issue. You determine just what the world is."

Banks and the Poor and Public TV.

The 1971 Public Television Conference at the Waldorf-Astoria in New York City awarded Joan Ganz Cooney its highly coveted first annual Ralph Lowell Medal for "the most extraordinary contribution to public broadcasting." I was wondering when they would get around to giving her some recognition for *Sesame Street*.

My own feeling is that Mort Silverstein, producer-writer of "Banks and the Poor," most deserved a medal in 1971. His documentary, analyzing how banking practices affect the poor, brought to the air what the commercial networks call "controversy." This had such an impact that the public television establishment decided not to have any more of that stuff.

The Public Broadcast Service (PBS), sponsor of the conference for the 204 noncommercial station managements it supplies with programs, was so turned off by the experiment that it refused to allow the producers (NET) to nominate "Banks and the Poor" for an Emmy. A study of the 487 pages of nominations submitted to the Academy of Television Arts and Sciences in 1971 shows that nothing on TV is too bad to be at least nominated. Mike Connors was nominated for his acting in Mannix, Sandy Koufax for his sports reporting, and so on. Thus, PBS' disdain for what many critics regarded the best documentary of the year arouses curiosity.

"Banks and the Poor" was scratched from public television's list of Emmy nominees and replaced by a program called "Turned-On Crisis." This was a model documentary in PBS' eyes. It was very fair. It presented both sides—con and pro—of the drug abuse problem. Not only that, President Nixon called it a terrific show and sent out a press release saying how much he liked it.

The controversial thesis of Silverstein's documentary was that banks have been taking advantage of the poor. He told us, for example, that self-respecting banks and savings and loan associations sometimes finance the finance companies that lend money at high interest rates to the very poor people the banks

15

turn away as bad credit risks. The bankers are also frequently the money men behind the home-improvement companies that have been known to fleece their customers. Many episodes of *The Young Lawyers* (ABC) and *Storefront Lawyers* (CBS) made the same points.

Nevertheless, the executives at PBS were very disturbed by Silverstein's show. One-sided documentaries about banking are bad. The rationale, perhaps, is that people might lose faith in banks and start stuffing their money under mattresses.

Silverstein undoubtedly assumed we all knew that bankers are benign, kindly, humane, helpful men—standing somewhere between doctors and social workers in the ranks of professionals who want to be our friends. Nothing, the TV commercials have been telling us for years, makes the average banker happier than the privilege of watching our money so we can all sleep better at night. Consequently, Silverstein didn't bother to give us the other side. His documentary made the bankers sound like ordinary American businessmen with recognizably human faults, including greed, close-fistedness, untrustworthiness, and a poorly developed social conscience.

Naturally, when for some reason PBS and local station managements showed the documentary in advance to banking groups across the nation, the bankers shrieked. And when the show actually went on the air, bankers by the dozens lost confidence in public television. A station in Los Angeles, it is said, lost a $50,000 pledge from one potential supporter, a banker. Other corporation presidents also joined the financial protest. Controversy seems to hit public television in the pocketbook. It's almost as bad as having sponsors.

With the loss of hefty donations, The Panic of 1970–71 was on. PBS couldn't simply fire the culprits. That would look too much like censorship. It decided to document what was wrong with the documentary.

At least PBS knew enough not to attempt the content analysis itself. That would be suspect. Somebody might think it was trying to tell its producers what they could not say, an indirect form of censorship. So PBS hired the equivalent of an independent research organization—a young university political scientist named Stephen Farber who nobody had heard of as an authority on journalism, television or banking. Not that his qualifications were that crucial. Basically, PBS wanted a report that would enable it to shriek in dismay: "What? Us guilty of one-sided reporting? Golly gee, that will never happen here again."

Within a few months Farber's official statement about the shortcomings of "Banks and the Poor" was in hand. It said that Silverstein's documentary was filled with sarcasm and irony. Farber added that it was often one-sided. Well, one didn't have to be a graduate student to recognize that. The best investigative reporting is almost always one-sided.

One point in Farber's report deserves special comment. Actually, Silverstein should comment on it, but since the report was secret and Silverstein hasn't seen it yet, I will take this opportunity to answer one of Farber's charges for him.

To Farber, the list of 123 congressmen with interests or directorships in banks, put on a crawl at the end of the documentary, was one of the most disturbing aspects of the show. "The list of congressmen," the secret report explains, "has the heading 'congressmen with bank holdings *or* serving as directors.' This is tantamount to saying: 'congressmen with speeding convictions *or* murder convictions.' . . . Everyone is lumped together as though all were guilty of some heinous crime." The compiling of the list, Farber adds, was "fifth-rate journalism."

I have been watching Silverstein's work on public television for years. His list may be third-rate journalism, or even fourthrate, but it is definitely not fifth-rate. The most impressive information revealed by the list, anyway, was the great number of men in Congress who are not personally involved in the industry they are responsible for regulating. How can the 300-odd legislators who don't have bank holdings know anything about the business without having a stake in it?

The Panic of 1970–71 was responsible for the "Standards of

Journalism" that PBS tried to get the station owners to adopt at the Waldorf-Astoria. Drawing from the lessons of "Banks and the Poor,' this document set forth guidelines on accuracy, completeness, objectivity, balance, and fairness. Those who saw the draft of the "Standards of Journalism" say it was inaccurate, incomplete, unobjective, unbalanced, and unfair. It even misspelled the name of Walter Lippmann.

The basic problem, it seems to me, is that public television is working at cross purposes to itself. It has a duty to perform in the public interest, which includes producing a number of controversial documentaries. But public television is supported by the financial and political establishments that are prime targets for documentaries. Charity, they say, begins at home. Anything that shakes public television's standing with its establishments is nothing PBS should get involved in.

Thomas Jefferson said an informed electorate is essential to the survival of our Republic. But what did he know about the problems of running a public television network?

A Baseball Game on TV. Definition: A show filled with those dramatic moments you wait hours to see.

Baseball Announcers. The baseball sportscasting business has never been the same since André Baruch, Red Barber's sidekick on the Brooklyn Dodger games, announced: "Pete Coscarart slides into second with a stand-up double."

Nowadays baseball journalism has been taken over by true professionals: ex-ball players themselves. As *Sports Illustrated* once observed, the scramble after these retired athletes "is the product of a mentality that would hire a patient to advise at his next operation."

The jock theory of TV sportscasting requires that stations hire athletes who are fairly good-looking and speak English. Ex-athletes are supposed to know things that non-athletes don't know. In practice they may know things, but if so, they don't tell you about them. They do speak English, but sometimes it sounds like a second language.

Basically, the ball player-sportscaster tells viewers things we usually have a pretty good idea about in advance. Frankie Frisch, for example, wrote the immortal line, "Oh, those bases on balls." That meant: It was better for a pitcher to have struck the fellow out, or have gotten him to fly or ground out, than to issue him a free ticket to first base. Those bases on balls can really kill you.

The amount of misinformation being handed out in TV sports journalism, I always assumed, was minimal. A postgame interview on a Sunday afternoon in 1971 (WOR-TV) makes me question even this advantage of the ball player-sportscaster.

Ralph Kiner, the No. 2 Mets' announcer, was interviewing Dock Ellis, the ace Pittsburgh Pirates pitcher, on "Kiner's Corner." "You had a good slider out there today," Kiner said. "No, I don't have a slider," Ellis answered. He mentioned several other pitches he did have.

"You really pitched out there today, anyway," Kiner went on. "No, I don't think I was too good out there," Ellis said of his victory against the Mets. "I didn't have my stuff today."

Kiner, 0–for–2 in the expertise league, was helped out of the jam by the start of the video tape replay part of the show. The first scene showed Ellis cutting off a ground ball. "You're a pretty good fielding pitcher out there," Kiner commented. "No, I'm not," Ellis said. "I just happened to get that one. I was in position. But I would say that fielding is one of my real weaknesses."

The video tape had showed a Met hitting a ball thrown by Ellis against the wall. "Was that a bad pitch, Dock?"

"I know you're supposed to say it's a bad pitch when they hit it like that," Ellis explained. "Well, I have to admit that this time it really was a bad pitch. A hanging curve. Like I said, I didn't have my stuff."

Kiner was 1–for–4. He laid the next one right down the middle for Ellis. "You look tall out there, Dock," Kiner said. "How tall are you?" Dock said he was six foot, three inches, proving Kiner hadn't lost his eye for height. "Certainly your biggest thrill," he continued, "has to be the no-hitter you threw against San Diego last year . . ."

Dock answered, "No, Ralph, my biggest thrill was the first major league game I appeared in. It was an exhibition game against Cleveland. I was called up from Kingston to pitch."

"That's in the Carolina League. That must have been some thrill," Kiner said. "That's right, Ralph," Ellis said. I scored two bingles for Kiner on that exchange, giving him 4–for–8 and a two-answer winning streak.

"This is your best season, Dock?"

"You can never tell this early in the year, Ralph."

"Well, you must feel that you have a thorough knowledge of the game now, in your third year?"

"No, I still have a long way to go, a lot of things to learn, Ralph."

That made it 4–for–10 on my scorecard, roughly the final score for the interview—a new major league broadcasting record!

Beauty Contests. I have a suspicion that the Women's Lib people, being mostly intellectual, haven't ever watched a beauty contest on television. There is something they should know about the genre. Beauty contests are the kind of show that starts at 10 o'clock at night. After it has been running for two hours, you look at your watch and it says 10:15 P.M. I don't know exactly what the producers of these extravaganzas do that is just right, but I don't want them to change their formula. Serious students of beauty contests never grow tired of looking at the same thing.

Beckett, Samuel. Samuel Beckett's play "Breath"

had its American premiere on the April 7, 1970 edition of "First Tuesday" on NBC. This was the first 35-second play by a Nobel Prize-winning dramatist ever to be presented on television in its entirety in this country.

One of the advantages of these shorter plays is that a critic can reprint the complete play and still have space to analyze it. "Breath," as staged at Oxford University, and first filmed by the BBC:

> The curtain rises. On stage center, piles of rubbish. Afterawhile, a baby's voice is heard. Crying. Afterawhile, there is a sigh. Afterawhile, the voice of the baby crying again. The curtain comes down.

Thus ends a most satisfying night in thirty-five second theatre, though in my opinion the play has entirely too much stage business to be completely successful. The dialogue is weak. There is no development of plot or character. But the play is not characterless. The baby's voice is that of everybaby, and evokes many emotions in anybody who has ever had one. "Breath" is rich in symbolism.

But the real value of Beckett's play is that it opens the door to experimentation in an area of television drama that needed encouragement. Everybody knows there are a lot of would-be playwrights who can't sustain a long play. The first act falls on its nose. Or the second act goes nowhere. Madison Avenue agencies, for example, are filled with dramatists who can write brilliantly in 25 words or less. Beckett's work legitimatizes this small area of theatre. Conversely "Breath" proves that Beckett may have a great future in advertising.

In the last analysis, "Breath" may just be too British for American television audiences. "It is an example of British understatement," explained Richard Lingeman, one of the many struggling American dramatists in the mini-play field.

To be able to write short plays well, according to Lingeman, the playwright needs a mini-talent. Most of Lingeman's unproduced work has been in 20-second plays. "You lose your audience if your play is any longer," Lingeman said. "The average adult who watches television has an attention span of ten seconds. Besides, you have to leave time for a spot commercial if you hope to sell a drama to the networks."

Lingeman works as an editor at the New York Times Book Review to subsidize his mini-play writing career. He decided to specialize in little shows ten years before Beckett. After being discharged from the army, he wrote a play called "Army Life":

> The curtain rises. Two soldiers are polishing shoes.
> 1st GI: (bleep).
> 2nd GI: What?
> 1st GI: (blipt).
> 2nd GI: Oh, I thought you said (bluck).

In the honors course in playwriting at Haverford, they had told Lingeman to write about what he knew. But the networks told him his play was not commercial, that he had to work within the existing structure of television. It was then that he wrote the first 20-second soap opera.

> ANNOUNCER: And now today's episode in "As the World Turns Through Dark Shadows We Search for Tomorrow in Peyton Place" . . . In yesterday's episode, while Carla was coming down from a bad LSD trip, David learned that Mrs. Davis was not really Dierdre's mother. David immediately went to Dr. Gleason and challenged his diagnosis of Clare's condition, leading Nurse Wynnecliffe to secretly phone George, who in turn phoned Lawrence, who was about to leave for San Diego to ship out with the Merchant Marine. And now today's episode . . .
> (Two men on the phone)
> FIRST MAN: Good bye, Lawrence.
> SECOND MAN: Good bye, George.
> ANNOUNCER: And so another eventful episode in the lives of the people in "As the World Turns Through Dark Shadows We Search for Tomorrow in Peyton Place."

Lingeman's dream is to form a production company, The Cliché Theatre, and present a regular live drama show on TV, called "Play of the Week." One of the scripts he has finished is "Commando Raid."

> An officer in World War II combat garb, his face smudged with dirt, is standing stage right.
> OFFICER: All right gentlemen, let's synchronize our watches. I make it 1400 hours minus five seconds. Four, three, two, one. Any questions? Yes, Forbush?
> FORBUSH: Is it 1400 hours when the big hand is on the 12 and the little hand is on two?
>
> CURTAIN

"Beckett is a breakthrough for all of us," Lingeman said.

Bill Buckley Gone Public. William F.

Buckley, the conservative superstar, officially became an intellectual when he moved his program, "Firing Line," from commercial television to public television in 1971. It always seemed that he had too many brains for commercial TV. You could tell that by his low ratings.

Traditionally, public television has small audiences. Station managements don't get hung up on materialistic things like sponsors. So the new Bill Buckley Hour—the show has not been retitled "Right On!"—should have no troubles on public TV.

Still, there are certain ironies in seeing a great champion of the free enterprise system turning to socialized television in order to stay on the air. Any Young American for Freedom knows that if a superstar can't make it on commercial television —the closest thing we have to the true marketplace Buckley is always talking about—he should accept the judgment of the public and get off the air.

I'd like to come to Buckley's defense on this point. Buckley's current situation is in the grand old conservative tradition of living off the government while knocking that practice. (Space limitations prevent my listing all the staunch conservatives receiving things like oil-depletion allowances and allotments for not planting crops while protesting the welfare state.)

In the meantime, the Corporation for Public Broadcasting, Buckley's new sponsor (with taxpayer money), must face another issue. Isn't he too controversial? CPB sources say that of the 100 stations presently carrying the syndicated "Firing Line," seventy are public television affiliates. So much for those who claim there's nothing controversial on public TV.

What happens now to CPB's widely publicized goal of balance? Since Ralph Nader's show was canceled, it would take a left-wing intellectual of Buckley's stature to restore the balance. I called I. F. Stone at his Washington office the other day to find out if he would be the star of "The Izzy Stone Hour."

"Why those yellow-bellied (bleeps)," Stone explained. "They have no (bleeps), no guts. What a way to prove public television's independence.

"Half the time public TV is kissing the Pentagon's (bleep) and running all that administration propaganda. Buckley's a rich man anyway. Why can't he subsidize his own show like all the other rich conservatives on the air. He could take out a second mortgage on his yacht or sell his polo ponies. Nobody ever subsidizes the left on TV."

Commercial TV has more courage than public TV, Stone says his experience proves. "I haven't thrown a bomb in several years," he explained. "The kids think of me as an old sellout. Yet the only time public TV has ever allowed me on the air, they had a *Reader's Digest* editor on to balance me out.

"If Jesus Christ came back to life on public television, they would put on Pontius Pilate and an M.I.T. professor to give the show balance. The moderator would be careful to explain the humane virtues of crucifixion. 'Sure, it's painful, but it's not as bad as burning at the stake.' By having Christ on, they'd be afraid of being unfair to the Roman authorities."

24

Blackouts.
Television stations' procedures for handling emergencies like transmitter power failures are inadequate. As the pictures fade from view, it would be helpful if the stations used their last ohms to flash a slide on the screen saying something reassuring like: "The remainder of the program is being canceled for lack of interest." As it was, during last summer's blackout, I thought King Kong had finally taken over the Empire State Building.

Black Week.
Four times a year, the rating services take a week off so all concerned can check their past figures, goof off, search their souls, or whatever those people do with their leisure time. Black Week, as this great institution is called, is believed to be a good thing. One TV luminary I know goes so far as to advocate a whole season of Black Weeks as an experiment. Then the networks would be able to put on all the great specials they dream of doing, on foreign policy or ecology, without fear of economic reprisals for low ratings. "Let the country learn something from TV for a change," explains the "Black Week Is Beautiful" proponent.

Black Week certainly gives the viewer the chance to see what the networks are capable of doing when not being watched. If the do-gooders are liberated, however, I don't think television would last a full season. The programmers went berserk last Black Week. For instance, they scheduled two documentaries in a row the same night.

The best way to see what the networks are capable of when they *are* being watched is during Sweeps Month. This is a little-known TV institution that occurs twice a year. Ratings services work especially hard during Sweeps Month, placing diaries in the homes of viewers in all the TV markets. Where the national Nielsen ratings try to find out in a general way which networks viewers are watching, the Sweeps try to find out exactly which

25

stations are being tuned in. Ad rates for the local stations are based on the Sweeps results.

According to the code of ethics governing American broadcasting, the networks are not supposed to do anything special in the way of programming to help their local affiliates at Sweeps time. They have to be honest. Otherwise the surveys would reflect only Sweeps Month and not the actual viewing during the whole season.

Still, you'll never see a documentary during the Sweeps unless it's about Liz Taylor or Marilyn Monroe. A Frank Sinatra special will always just happen to be scheduled in a Sweeps Month. A Maxwell Smart is apt to have twins right in the middle of the Sweeps. A Fred MacMurray will finally get married during the Sweeps. *The Sound of Music* plays twice a year on TV, both times during the Sweeps. When *Gone With the Wind* or *The Stewardesses* comes to TV, you can be sure it will be during a Sweeps period.

Someday I hope to get to the bottom of why all this happens. Any isolated period of time in which ratings are not taken, it seems, brings out the worst in broadcasting people. Any isolated period in which ratings are certain to be taken tends to bring out the best in broadcasting people. There may not be too much difference between the two extremes. But if I had my druthers—which, of course, nobody gets in TV—I'd rather have a whole season of Sweep Months than Black Weeks. It would be interesting to see what would happen if the networks had to hang by their thumbs for a whole season.

Bleep. (See also "Blip"). One of the things television does better than any other medium is censoring. It's hardly noticeable, as this transcript suggests.

ANNOUNCER: And now for a frank discussion of the New Obscenity—the dirty words, the filth, and smut which have found their way into so much contemporary language. What do you think, Professor? Do you condone the use of such words as (bleep)?

PROFESSOR: Well, of course (bleeping) is something which everybody does. Of course you don't have to call (bleeping) (bleeping). You can always call it (buzzing).

ANNOUNCER: (Angrily). I told you this was a family program. What the (bleep) do you think you're doing?

The word *bleep* is actually a misnomer, which harks back to the early days of television when offensive material was covered over with a loud bleeping sound. The disadvantage of that method of censorship gradually became obvious: It called attention to the censor's heavy hand. Today the censoring process should more accurately be called silencing.

Blip. (See also "Bleep"). The current rise of obscenity in the university, theater, movies, and other entertainment arts has left television far behind. But then the medium's strength has never been in presenting an accurate picture of life. After a spate of complaints about too much violence on TV, the industry stopped showing make-believe violence. Instead, it increased its coverage of actual brutality on news shows. Seeing real people killed on real battlefields during dinner no longer makes viewers lose their appetites.

The use of four-letter words in commercial television, however, is still largely limited to shows like Johnny Carson's and Dean Martin's. If a studio audience seems to be falling asleep, the host or one of his guests throws in a dirty word or joke. The network censors always edit the blue material from Johnny or Dino's program, but it sure wakes the studio audience up.

The best way to prepare the public for the language revolution is to discuss obscenity intelligently, in a mature and rational forum. Prurient interest can be better doused by the panel discussion than by any other art form on the medium. An interesting experiment, showing how boring obscenity can become, was conducted in the spring of 1971 at New York's municipal educational television station, WNYC-TV.

Steve Scheuer, the host of a talk show called "All About TV," invited a number of experts to speak frankly about television's most embarrassing problem. The panel included Fred Bohlen of the Ford Foundation; Jack White, ex-president of NET; Richard Schickel, the *Life* magazine critic; Marie Greco of the Columbia School of Journalism faculty; and Fred Wiseman, the filmmaker whose documentary, "Hospital," won an Emmy.

"All About TV" was to be the first program to tell us all about censorship. The program used as a visual aid Wiseman's film-essay "Law and Order," parts of which appeared on the Public Broadcast Laboratory (PBL) in 1968. This recorded a day in the life of the Kansas City Police Department, focusing on the prosaic arrest of several black kids charged with car theft. It shows the cops breaking into an apartment looking for the alleged thieves. A few moments later, the kids are apprehended in a back alley; a melee follows.

In the two-minute sequence (as originally filmed) the kids use the expression "motherfucker" eighteen times. They also promise the policemen they will "kill a cop for them someday." But in the version shown on PBL, the police seem suddenly agitated, starting to bang the kids' heads against a parked car for no apparent reason. That was because PBL, in its infinite wisdom, decided Wiseman's report had to be edited. They cut half a word eighteen times. What experimental TV fans thus heard in the two minutes on the home screen was "mother(blip)," eighteen times.

One could argue that this was a militantly moderate approach to truth in TV journalism. It was experimental enough to use the word "mother," but not experimental enough to use the second half. Besides, everybody knows what "mother" stands for.

Wiseman contended that the cuts had destroyed the impact

28

of the scene. "Without hearing the swearing," he claimed, "you don't approve of the cops' strange behavior. There's no motivation in the scene. If it had been played as it happened, you still may not agree with what they did. But at least it showed the cops had a reason to be incensed. They were going to cut out a few 'Jesus Christs' and 'damns.' I yelled and screamed about those, too, and they left them in."

The filmmaker's protests were not altogether in vain. After "Law and Order" was shown, the anchorman on the PBL show that night announced that cuts were made over the objection of the filmmaker.

Wiseman recounted this background material during the discussion on "All About TV." Two of the men who made the decision to censor his film happened to be sitting on the panel. Usually hatchet men will say the film was too long; they had to cut somewhere, so they left out the obscenities. But Fred Bohlen, at that time the head of PBL, said he ordered the film cut because he didn't want the educational television stations to drop the whole show in the belief that their viewers would find the one sequence objectionable. Jack White, who knew the minds of educational TV station management better than anyone, explained that he didn't like censorship, but was concerned about the affiliates' sensibilities.

The debate over "Law and Order" was followed by a literate discussion about the propriety of using the word "fuck" on television. The majority of panelists agreed there was nothing wrong with such usage. It was a first in television history, a step forward in the medium's growth.

Actually, it wasn't so much a step forward as a step sideways. After the show was finished, it was not aired.

Some hail this decision as television's ultimate statement on censorship.

Boobs. NBC executives are still studying the tapes of Ann-Margret's appearance on "The Johnny Carson Show."

That's understandable; I've never heard so many different eye-witness accounts of an accident on TV. At the risk of making a molehill out of a mountain, I pieced together what really happened.

Ann-Margret was on her way to a Hollywood party in a beautiful red dress that looked like an old-fashioned man's undershirt. As an accessory, she wore a shawl. The all-seeing NBC cameras covered her pre-party entrance and walk across stage to give the standard hello kiss to the host. As she faced the audience and made her way to the couch, the accident occurred.

The shawl either fell or jumped from her shoulders. While just standing there, everything was fine. But trouble started when the actress sat down. It was what the industry likes to call "event television."

One eyewitness viewer with perfect eyes says the report that Ann-Margret was completely exposed is absurd. He saw two strings the thickness of thread shielding the actress' bosom. Viewers who turned their eyes to see if their wives were watching before looking at things like that, missed the event. Before you could say "General Sarnoff," the NBC cameras suddenly focused on Ann-Margret's adam's apple.

Carson, who reportedly has seen everything, rubbed his eyes with the heel of his right hand and carried on as if nothing unusual had happened. He asked his guest if she was going to a party like *that*. She was. "Well, if you can wear a dress like that in public," he said, "it's a shame we can't show it on television."

I'm sure it was a perfectly normal dress for a woman of Ann-Margret's position—a movie star—to wear to a party. But before we get preoccupied with the kind of party she was going to, I should point out that not everybody buys the accident theory.

Why did Ann-Margret choose to wear her most alluring party clothes? It may be that she was fearful nobody would pay attention to her if she wore some simple covered-up number, like the dress the noted conversationalist Raquel Welch recently wore on "The Dick Cavett Show."

Ann-Margret received an enormous amount of free publicity

that night. But it's sad to think that when presented with an enormous audience of millions she couldn't come up with anything better than baring her breasts.

"Carson's argument was very weak," the NBC censor explained. "We don't care if Ann-Margret goes to parties naked. But the public's not going to the party." The censors' argument seems very weak. The reason Carson goes to Hollywood is to show us how the natives live. They are worth studying on TV after midnight as much as the natives of New Guinea who walk around much the same way in National Geographic specials.

The British Pause.
One of the oddest things about British television is that for as many as ten or twelve hours a day there is nothing on the air. Of course, they have the test card (test pattern). BBC-1 has been running the same picture of a cute ten-year-old girl since 1959. And there is classical and popular music to watch the test pattern by.

A lot of British people leave the set on for warmth, a sensible thing to do in a country where central heating hasn't caught on like TV. But there are still those long dreary hours of the day and night when there are no programs on. It's really appalling.

Looking into this quirk of British television, I found that they have the know-how to keep their stations going virtually twenty-four hours a day, as many American stations do. The British seem to practice remarkable restraint in not filling the time. Their minister of posts and tele-communications, who regulates the medium by law, fixes program hours at fifty-three and one-half hours a week for BBC-1 and thirty-two hours a week for BBC-2 (the egghead channel).

How can an Englishwoman take it? One notices packs of children actually *playing* outside in the morning and afternoon, for God's sake. A lot of kids also waste their time reading.

Going dark—as the artistic principle is called in the theater

—would seem to be a creative experiment the American networks might try some year. "It will never work," explained one industry veteran to whom I've broached the idea. "The networks are saying that if the viewer was allowed to walk away for an hour or two, he would never come back. It's against human nature."

B.S-G. (Before the Surgeon-General).

In the days before cigarette advertising on TV was prohibited, I went to visit Young & Rubicam on Madison Avenue to study, without the usual pause for the programs, one of the season's most culturally intriguing campaigns: the L&M commercials, based on the theme "There *IS* a cigarette for the two of you."

Y&R won fame for its socially-conscious "Give a Damn" commercials for the New York Urban Coalition. When the agency won its first big cigarette account a few seasons back, everybody in the field was wondering how they would cope with the creative problem of turning people on to cigarettes.

The curtain rises in the most widely-seen of the L&M commercials with a woman saying, "Tony." A man answers, "Ummm." "I had a dream about you," she says, ending the first act.

There are a lot of long shots of mysterious buildings, and short shots of mysterious people in dinner clothes conducting serious dialogue in broad daylight. It seemed vaguely familiar. Finally I remembered: it was *Last Year at Marienbad* again, condensed to sixty seconds, a cultural triumph. The original film was too long in its three-hour version.

"It's Fellini directing," I said to the Y&R account executive at my side as the commercial unreeled.

"Richard Lester," he explained. "The man who did the Beatles' *Hard Day's Night*. We shot at Cliveden. You know. In England."

The man in the before-six tuxedo began the second act by asking the woman in a diaphanous gown, "Was it sad?" As a

dream interpretation buff, I jotted down the remainder of the dialogue for future analysis:

> She: I'm not sure.
> He: Tell me about it .
> She: All right. You were away and you were writing to me. You had a rubber stamp and stamped every one of your letters with a big, red *Love*, as though the word was just a social amenity. Like saying, "Bless you," when you sneeze.
> He: Is that it?
> She: Just about. What do you think?
> He: Well, I think we ought to talk about it.

By the time the voice-over finished saying, "There *IS* a cigarette for the two of you," I had it interpreted as just another sex dream.

"Well, what do you think?" a Y&R publicity woman at my other elbow asked when the curtain came down. "Beautiful," I said.

In advertising jargon today, that means that an $80,000 commercial by a famous director like Richard Lester is just okay. He brought the commercial in at sixty seconds on the button. The cinematic values were there. Everything was okay except the dialogue, which left something to be desired.

33

What did this fantastic drama between two people who acted like catatonics have to do with selling cigarettes?

The agency people explained that the idea behind the campaign was to give L&M an identity. Unlike smokers of Marlboros, Tareytons, Winstons and Camels, when an L&M smoker was asked what his cigarette meant to him, "He just looked out of the window." By showing two people of opposite sex puffing on the same cigarette, Y&R, had, at last, achieved the image of bisexualism. In sixty seconds, I guess, they had doubled the sales potential over either the masculine or feminine brand cigarettes.

I coughed politely, and the second commercial in the series came on the screen. It showed a couple having an argument coming out of a 42nd Street movie theater, with the same happy ending.

"Beautiful," I said. "That Lester can really handle crowd scenes."

"John Schlesinger," the Y&R man explained. "He's the one who directed *Midnight Cowboy*."

The third commercial turned out to be the work of another great director, Carol Reed of *The Loves of Isidora*. It was also beautiful.

Admittedly cigarettes are a tough subject to say anything good about in commercials these days.

"We'd like to think of them as mini-movies," the Y&R spokesman explained. "That's why we got such great directors to give their impressions of how a cigarette can bring people together."

He wasn't smoking. Neither was I. The money it cost to hire top directors doesn't come out of anybody's pocket except L&M smokers'. So the expensive Y&R campaign isn't without redeeming social value.

The Bull-Running on Madison Avenue. There's been a scurrilous rumor floating around about the new Merrill Lynch commercial. That's the one

in which the voice of Kevin McCarthy—who TV viewers will recall played the crooked banker in ABC's "The Survivors"—explains: "America . . . Merrill Lynch is bullish about America."

Merrill Lynch, the rumor says, was so bullish about America that it used Mexican bulls in the inspirational message about the economy. "The nicest thing that can be said about the commercial is that it's stupid," explained one ad agency president. "Maybe it's also dishonest."

"I can't believe that an upstanding brokerage house would use anything but the finest American bulls, sir," I told the rumor-monger. "Why would they go to Mexico to shoot a commercial about the American economy?"

"Do you think they're crazy?" my Madison Avenue source explained. "Everything is so expensive in this country."

It turned out that Merrill Lynch's agency, Ogilvy & Mather, *did* use Mexican bulls. But not because they were selling the American economy short or trying to save a few pesos in getting across how smart it is to invest in America.

"Mexican bulls look better on film," explained a spokesman for Ogilvy & Mather. "The creative people decided we had to use only black fighting bulls. American herds aren't all black, at least the ones we saw. They have dun-colored bulls mixed in. Sometimes those creative people stretch a gnat's ass over a barrel in their search for perfection.

"The other consideration was that we had to get the open prairie look in the commercial. As the bulls come over the horizon, we didn't want anything to distract the viewer. The horizon couldn't be visually interesting, you know, with beautiful mountains looming, like in the Southwest."

Capitol Crime Critics.

A review of the 1971–2 TV season was published in my favorite humor magazine, *The Congressional Record.* "A full twenty of the fifty-six prime-time hours of our three major networks are occupied by detective shows—blind detectives, fat detectives, private detectives and detectives upholding the honor of local, state and federal governments," explained the government's newest TV critic, Senator Robert Byrd (D–W. Va.). "If our streets were as amply patrolled as our prime TV hours, we could all sleep a lot better at night."

First, I want to clear up the notion that we can all sleep better at night because the streets on our TV sets are amply protected. A total of seventy-eight people were killed right in front of my eyes last week.

Six women were strangled in their homes in Honolulu on "Hawaii Five-O" one week in 1971 by a pervert who painted their faces with cosmetics. I know that sort of thing has been going on for years out there in Hawaii on TV. But in past seasons the stranglings took place off camera. In 1971–2 they showed us the actual stranglings.

Senator Byrd, what many amateur critics like yourself probably don't understand is why the networks have a commitment to this kind of programming in the first place. *Variety,* our trade paper, recently theorized it dates back to a night four years ago when Mort Werner, NBC's vice president of programming, was mugged while waiting for a commuter train at 125th Street. Brooding about his busted nose, he ran into one of the big wheels of Hollywood justice—Jack Webb—and ordered a spin-off of "Dragnet," called "Adam–12." The cycle, explained *Variety,* just grew. Completely forgotten was the possibility that Werner's mugger might have been inspired by an earlier NBC crime show.

I should warn you, Senator Byrd, that if you ask the networks about the rise of crime shows on TV, they won't even know what you are talking about. There are no crime shows on TV, only "action-adventure" shows.

If you were to ask them why there has been a rise of violence in action-adventure shows, they would answer, "Life is full of violence."

Then they would say that you shouldn't take action-adventure shows seriously. They are escapist entertainment, designed to take TV viewers' minds off the reality of all the violence in American society. This is especially difficult to understand: Shouldn't a guy who has just been mugged on his way home from work, or a woman who has just been raped, want to escape from reality with make-believe fiction?

Car Salesman of the Year. As we all know, insincerity is no barrier to success in this country. A character in the movie *Joe* sees a famous old political poster which asks the question: "Would you buy a used car from this man?" "Of course," he says. "Why not, he's the president of the United States." Of all professions, the car salesman is almost a metaphor for dishonesty.

It's this great tradition of slightly suspicious car salesmen that seems to explain American Motors' decision to hire Kevin McCarthy as TV spokesman for its 1971 line of beautiful cars.

McCarthy was last seen on the medium as the unsuccessful banker in Harold Robbins' series, "The Survivors."

However, the opening scene in McCarthy's commercial for American Motors is more reminiscent of *Patton*. He's standing with his hands on his hips under the largest flag in TV commercial history. It serves as a patriotic backdrop for McCarthy's apparently sincere discussion about why we should buy American Motors' cars. As he speaks, however, I can't forget the last time I saw McCarthy on TV.

For twenty-six weeks last season, he was the shifty, opportunistic financier who married the daughter of the world's smartest banker (Lana Turner, who was pregnant by some other man). He played around with other women, was a rotten father to his illegitimate child, tried to gain control of the family bank by lying, cheating, blackmailing, embezzling, and ultimately almost got away with murder. McCarthy is a terrific actor.

As first glance, he seems to have changed a lot since a depression in the ratings closed the Carlyle Bank. His hair is long now, he has a drooping mustache (the first Detroit spokesman ever to wear one on camera) and he is clad in a youthful-looking beige suit and boots (underneath the suit). But as soon as he says, "We at American Motors . . ." one senses that he hasn't changed that much.

The creative director at Wells, Rich & Green who hired the spokesman confirms that McCarthy hasn't retired as an actor and become an executive in Detroit. It was just a figure of speech, the agency man explained.

Wells, Rich & Green, the advertising agency, had to test more than fifty top actors in Hollywood and New York before they could find the right man for the job. "It had to be someone who seemed involved," they explained, "someone who had the right power of conviction, a strong personality, a man who represented not only youth but had strength and dynamic qualities with which when he says these things makes you believe in them. Kevin was the only one who had this kind of concern."

Kevin McCarthy may be personally charming, truly dedicated

to his family off-camera, and have the highest ethical values. But none of these things seem to get in the way of his work for American Motors. Not only does he appear appropriately insincere, but he manages to project just the right shifty, sleazy, crooked approach. He is the super car salesman of the generation.

All the commercials in the American Motors series end with McCarthy asking a question: "What would you do, if you had to compete with the three biggest car companies?" "Fire Kevin McCarthy," some might say. If I were an advertising genius, like Mary Wells Lawrence, I'd recommend that American Motors reduce its ad budget drastically and plow the money back into basic research. The little fellow in Detroit who invents a car that will last as long as the 1948 models did, won't need a sharpie on TV to move them out of the showroom.

China: TV Tells It Like It Is. For the
last twenty years, I sat in front of the TV set watching the networks reporting about the struggle between Chiang Kai-shek and Mao Tse-tung, and my brain was washed and dried. Before I knew what was happening, the ring around my ideological collar about China was gone.

It made so much sense to be a dedicated anti-Communist in those days. All the networks were saying that Communism was bad for the people of China. I was weak and didn't want to read a book or anything to find out about what was really going on over there. I was such an innocent dupe, I even doubted that Mao knew how to swim.

The networks' coverage of the president's visit to China (February, 1972) has convinced me that being hard on Communism all these years was a serious error in judgment. I was immature and didn't know what I was doing by falling under the spell of TV's manipulators. (Most outsiders knew that twenty percent of the TV newsmen were Communists, but what they didn't know was that eighty percent were anti-Communists.)

39

In my defense, I can only say that I was never an active member of the anti-Communist movement. I mean, I never played an important role in the anti-Communist conspiracy or anything.

To the best of my recollection, I never once preached or taught the violent overthrow of the People's Republic of China. Why, I even thought John Foster Dulles was out of his mind when he advocated unleashing Chiang Kai-shek. As soon as his Nationalist troops reached the mainland, I was sure they would walk home. And I was afraid that if we ever conquered the mainland, as a member of the Army Reserve, I would be called back to active duty for the remainder of my life as one of the 80,000,000 GI's needed to occupy defeated China. I was, in retrospect, just another hack anti-Communist who merely did what almost every TV viewer was doing the past twenty years: believing in the Red Menace.

Why am I the first anti-Communist TV critic to confess in full detail his role in the anti-Communist movement? If the thaw in Chinese–American relations continues, one day soon I expect to be called before the House Un-American Activities Committee and be asked the question I've dreaded since I decided to quit the movement when I saw President Nixon standing on the Great Wall: "Are you now, or have you ever been, an anti-Communist?"

Cinemascope on TV (What You're Missing):

Here's a simple fool-proof
method of detecting when
the TV networks are gypping
you out of seeing a whole
movie, like "Ben-Hur,"
which I learned while watching
"Cleopatra." ICHARD BURTON
was listed in the credits.

So was
the famous
he is better—
JOSEPH MANKIEWICZ.
TV will never
And so it
HE END.
enjoyed "Ben Hur"
the other night,
of it. Didn't
those loin cloths
For me
often gets in
the story in
"Cleopatra," I
whether we
Alexandria.
nothing confusing
race in "Hur."
year to build
time than the
worked faster
The arena set
acres. MGM
feet of lumber;
million pounds
25,000 miles
tons of white
in from
The race sequences
months to film.
the chariot race
runaway in
This must have
disappointing to
who bet on

OSEPH MANKIEW,
director (although
known as
USIC COMPOSED BY [?]
tell you.
goes, until
I really
(Part II)
what there was
you just love
by Edith Head?
the spectacle
the way of
spectaculars. In
never knew
were in Rome or
But there was
about the chariot
It took a
the track, more
original. Labor
in the old days.
covered 18 square
used 40,000 cubic
more than a
of plaster, and
of tubing; 40,000
sand were carted
Mediterranean beaches.
alone took three
But on TV
looked like a
Central Park.
been very
all the people
the race at OTB.

41

The real reason
aired only the
films, a reliably
at a rival
is because
will be a
next month,
side the month
is Liz's
still be on
up-coming
In the remaining
"Ben Hur"
teeth will be
attraction.
TV is a

ABC and CBS
center of their
informed source
network told me,
the left side
full-length feature
and the right
after. Only thing
breasts will
camera in both
ABC super-specials.
two episodes of
Charlton Heston's
the center
"Ben Hur" on
two-ring circus.

Civilisation.

If you ask the average intellectual if he watches "Bonanza" or "Gunsmoke," he will say, "No, of course not. But once I did see an episode. You remember the one where Hoss got the croup?" It often turns out they know the plot lines of ninety-seven percent of the westerns.

All of my intellectual friends said they watched "Civilisation" last season. But every time I try to have an intelligent discussion about what Lord Clark said in the eighth or twelfth lecture, they don't seem to have watched that one.

I can't confirm this rumor since I haven't seen them either, but there are those who say the last twelve installments of "Civilisation" were filled with beautiful color slides of Lord Clark's wife and other great relics, his kids posing along the Roman viaducts and playing cricket in front of the great cathedrals.

Lord Clark's review of western culture from the fall of the

Roman Empire to the twentieth century is popular with local station managers because it won't get them into trouble. It is one of the least controversial shows in the history of Public TV. Anybody who complains about "Civilisation" is obviously a hopeless barbarian.

The structure of "Civilisation"—it divides twenty centuries into thirteen parts of fifty-two minutes each—creates some continuity problems. If you are called to the telephone or to the bathroom, you miss two centuries.

A Classic Documentary. The classic way to make a one-hour television documentary is to present a mass of material on a broad subject. In the last minute or so, the narrator tells the viewer: "You've just seen everything we could find on the subject. Now you decide what to think about it." Following this general pattern, television has helped end hunger, poverty, pollution, migratory labor, cigarette smoking, and the war in Vietnam.

Controversy and Public Television.

It's not easy to define controversy on commercial television; one's station's controversy is another's banality. In public television, however, there is a convenient index. You always know something is controversial when the educational station managements refuse to carry the show. They tend to be liberal on carrying shows like tennis championships (about eighty percent of the PBS affiliates ran it) and conservative on shows like the Bobby Seale interview (thirty percent ran it).

The final solution for dealing with controversy would be for PBS to work out an arrangement whereby the British Broadcasting Corporation did all of its investigative reporting about American society.

Kenneth Clark is not controversial, although his "Civilisation" was one of the most one-sided shows ever produced (ask any Moslem or Oriental historian). Kenneth Clark's "Civilisation in Banking," Kenneth Clark's "Civilisation in Washington," Kenneth Clark's "Civilisation in the Ghettos," Kenneth Clark's "Civilisation in the Pentagon Public Information Office," Kenneth Clark's "Civilisation in the FBI"—all done with his usual witty comments and traditional British understatement— would put an end to charges of biased reporting. PBS could always fall back on the standard disclaimer that any similarity between the opinions expressed by the BBC and PBS is purely coincidental.

Corporation for Public Broadcasting.

The Corporation for Public Broadcasting was set up by an act of Congress to serve as a buffer agency, an instrument for guaranteeing that when the government handed over taxpayer money to run public TV, political influence wouldn't be felt at the local-station level. Congress guarded against political influence by allowing the White House to fill the CPB board with presidential appointees. That way, Congress could apply pressure against a cultural bureaucracy, instead of directly against the local stations.

CPB was supposed to collect money from a diversity of sources, an additional protection from political influence. But it's a lot easier raising the money from a single large source, such as the federal treasury, than a lot of small foundations. The ratio so far has been roughly 15,000,000 federal dollars for each million of private dollars.

This process works very well on public television. The Ralph Nader show gets dropped because of low ratings. William F. Buckley is the season's hot new act. There are no documentaries exposing the government, such as "The Selling of the Pentagon."

Perhaps the conservatives in Congress would be smarter to forget about out-takes and work behind the scenes to force CBS to accept a little taxpayer money. With the recession and all, it might just work.

Cosell, Howard. See "Presidential Press Conferences."

Crass Commercialism. The news that ABC is proposing to reduce by half the number of commercials per hour on its Saturday morning kiddy shows was particularly depressing. I don't care how many awards President James Duffy of ABC-TV wins for his outrageously anti-American-broad-

casting-system speech to the ABC affiliates in Martinique. Cutting down on commercials, I submit, is not what commercial broadcasting is all about. Crass commercialism is. As far as I am concerned, the networks are not commercial enough, especially in children's programming.

One of the reasons for this rise in crass public servicism is that nobody gives the broadcasters awards for being crassly commercial—they just give money. Although some people feel money is its own reward, broadcasters also want awards. They live for recognition.

To meet this need, I have decided to sponsor a new award to encourage creativity in making a buck out of broadcasting. It is called the Mammy, named after the great god Mammon, who has always guided television artistically and without credit. An example of great achievement in commercial broadcasting that went unsung in the past because there weren't any Mammys was the invention of the Sixty-Second Injury in TV football games. The purpose of this innovation was to create an artificial timeout in the game so the networks could insert a commercial while a poor fellow lay writhing on the ground.

This shouldn't be confused with the Twenty-Second Injury, introduced in NBA basketball games on TV. These delays for shorter commercials are caused by shoelaces coming untied, according to schedules worked out by a network's sales departments.

The Sixty-Second Injury really helped broadcasting while doing absolutely nothing for football. As a matter of fact, the pause for the commercial actually may have hurt the game, since it gives players time to catch their breath. They shouldn't have time to do that. If the brains who thought up football wanted anybody to catch his breath, they would have thought of it without TV's help. Extra commericals may be one of the reasons there are so many upsets in TV football today.

These artificial timeouts are such a wonderful example of the basic principle commercial broadcasting was built on—he who pays the piper calls the tune—it may even deserve higher recognition than a mere Mammy. This super-Mammy should be called the Golden Calf Award (or Caffy). (The last time the networks did anything truly worth of a Caffy was in 1965, when CBS first thought of the idea of having seven minutes of commercials per hour in its movies, instead of six.)

The American educational system just doesn't produce enough men who are thinking along the crassly commercial lines that made commercial broadcasting great. Hopefully, the Mammys and Caffys will spur the industry on to new heights.

As a starter, a Mammy should be given to every TV station in the U.S. Just for being. This automatically solves the problem faced by the stations who have no commendations in their files to show the FCC when they come up for license renewal.

The Crawl. Everybody who works for television agrees that the ideal presentation of the list of credits at the end of a show took place on the Academy Awards telecast of 1954 or 1955. That was the night Jerry Lewis was the host, *Gigi* was the best picture of the year, and the business of handing out the Oscars ended twenty-two minutes ahead of time.

The credits were run rather slowly the first time. Jerry Lewis put more cigarettes in his nose than even he knew what to do with, and he still had twenty minutes left to fill. Eventually the "crawl"—as the professionals call the rotating drum which holds all the names of those involved in bringing the wonderful program to us—ran eleven times.

The opposite extreme in presentation of the credits was recently cited by the Federal Communications Commission, who complained that NBC and ABC were flashing those "promotional consideration furnished by" lines—the highlight for crawl-readers interested in muckraking—too fast. They were flying by at such a rapid rate of speed last year, the FCC ruled, that the small-type visual announcements "seem to obscure rather than reveal that payments have been made for advertising purposes."

Some veteran crawl-readers long ago had gathered from the credits that couldn't be read by the human eye that the networks were trying to slip one over on them. Perhaps the crawl-operators didn't want them to know that a mighty corporate symbol of responsibility in communications would stoop to such penny-ante stuff as trading their integrity for a few free suitcases, a crummy motel room, or a coach ride on an almost empty late night airplane flight.

Recipients of the free advertising weren't too happy about the development of the fireball crawl. It was also frowned on by the ordinary working people whose names are featured on the crawl. They live for the moment at the end of the show when millions can see their names in the equivalent of lights. Some television people I know only watch that part of a show.

All of which must come as something of a surprise to many viewers who always thought the list of credits was a meaningless ritual. Opinions about the crawl cover the spectrum from "boring" to "tedious." Actually, there is almost as much experimentation going on in the last minute or so of most shows than in the part people usually watch.

Much of what we see today on TV in the way of crawls is inspired by the movies. The credits usually come on one at a time, like the sun rising in the south and sinking in the north. Still other times they come on in groups of three. Occasionally there is a promo for the next show behind the list of credits. "Watch 'Nanny & the Professor,'" a voice says. "When Timmie has a toothache. Next." That's the equivalent of running scenery behind the credits in the movies.

One of the more interesting developments lately is the writing of original material for the crawl. Tom Whedon and David Axlerod—two of the writers featured on the crawl of "The Dick Cavett Show" (ABC) every night—have been trying to improve the entertainment value of the list of credits by adding an occasional note of levity.

48

Whedon and Axlerod's first line—"Mosquitoes by Marsh"—premiered in March, 1968, but was never reviewed by the critics. That is the lot of crawl writers.

Serious students of the art form, however, will never forget such later Whedon-Axlerod classics as "Mr. Cavett's gowns by Cecil," "The Talking Horse was Pre-Recorded," and "Moral Guidance for Mr. Cavett Supplied by the Moral Guidance Club of Secaucus, N. J."

Whedon and Axlerod have finished writing a number of lines which should appear on the Cavett credits in the near future. To encourage the growth of crawl-reading, they gave me a preview last week. A few coming attractions: "Tonight's Dick Cavett Show Was Adapted from a Short Story by Nikolai Gogol." "The Tribute to Rutherford B. Hayes Was Spontaneous and Unrehearsed." "The Color Yellow Courtesy of the Spectrum."

The Curse of ABC. The Curse of ABC originated on "Dark Shadows," which was canceled in 1971 after four years of meeting the daytime needs of the supernatural audience. A Gothic soap opera, it had one of the most mentally challenging story lines in the history of the medium. Characters went back

in time to 1890 and 1840 without warning. Still other times they slipped into the third dimension for no apparent reason. That dimension had rarely been used in soap opera.

"Dark Shadows" was also extremely romantic. "More so than 'Love Story,' " explained Bill Reynolds, a leading authority. "The relationships were very strong, powerful, sweeping yet tragic. It was romantic in the sense of 'Ivanhoe.' "

When ABC decided to kill "Dark Shadows," a major problem was resolving all the plots—covering a period of 161 years—at Collinwood, the ancestral manse. The mop-up took three weeks, beginning with the resolving of Barnabas, that handsome, suave vampire played by Jonathan Frid. The ladies at home found him irresistible, it has been said, because he was the last word in dangerous males. He was the nice guy beset with vampirism, something like a romantic hero plagued with bouts of malaria. Suddenly at this late date the witch who originally turned Barnabas into a vampire fell in love with him and, in self preservation, she took away his instinct for the jugular. She in turn was mysteriously shot.

But the resolution of the loose ends didn't begin in earnest until the final chapter. There, within 30 minutes, everybody died, became sane, or got married. That was quite an accomplishment, made possible by the end of the Curse that had plagued Collinwood since 1841.

The happy ending was marred only by the fact that the Curse of Collinwood had to go somewhere: something to do with the balance of the supernatural. All the authorities that I've consulted agree that the Curse descended on ABC. "Except for Mr. Cavett," Mr. Reynolds explained.

The Curse of the ABC was to center on Alan Ludden, the host of "Password," the game show replacing "Dark Shadows." "Don't be surprised if whenever he steps into the overhead lights," the Keeper of the Curse predicted, "he begins to turn into Wolfman."

Cwizlicki, Gus. See "Rockefeller, John D. III."

Day, Doris. My doctor won't let me watch "The Doris Day Show." I have a family history of diabetes.

Daytime Politics. The networks have taken all kinds of polls to find out what the public wants. The one thing all the polls agree on is that the public doesn't want politics on TV. However, peoples' ideas in a democracy are always changing.

We are not interested in politics now. But that may be because television, with its enormous potential for educating the public, has not been trying especially hard to keep us informed about politics. All they give us are political speeches, the most boring aspect of politics. Even politicians don't listen to each other's speeches. If we spent six hours a day watching politicians performing in their committee rooms and cloakrooms in Washington, I suspect politics would be much more interesting.

Anybody who watched a show like "Dark Shadows" in the afternoon would be fascinated by the creepy machinations of Congress. An interest in politics may be an acquired taste, something that can be developed like an interest in soap opera. Who can say that the level of political sophistication can't also rise some day?

The Double Standard in Reruns.

Aida premiered November 12, 1886, at the old Metropolitan Opera House. Since then there have been 556 reruns.

All my friends who are opera buffs tell me that's good. In fact, it's so good that many of our leading citizens are asking the government to subsidize the 557th rerun with taxpayer money.

David Merrick took a full-page ad in the *New York Times* September 9, 1970, proudly announcing that *Hello Dolly!*, in playing its 2,718th performance at the St. James Theater, had broken the record for the longest-running musical. That's one original, according to my calculations, and 2,717 reruns.

My neighborhood movie house ran a picture last week. It was the same one they reran the week before. And the week before that.

Educational television always reruns its programs during the season, sometimes twice in one week. "Sesame Street" sometimes consists of five reruns in a week.

The only medium that really gets criticized for reruns, however, seem to be commercial television. Well, the double standard isn't fair, and I've decided to come to the aid of the poor networks.

The first thing they ought to do is find a new name for what they do in the summer. With the ecology craze, I suggest they call it "recycling." Recycled programs, they should explain, are a great public service. "The average network original program telecast between September and April had a nineteen-household rating," explained a researcher at NBC named Sheldon Jacobs, who has volunteered to work with me on this project to rehabiliate the networks' good name. "In plain English this means in nineteen percent of the households, one or more persons saw that program."

If you think about it for a while, it also means that eighty-one percent of the households did not see the original telecast. Shouldn't this eighty-one percent get a chance to see a show, just as *Hello, Dolly!* ran until everybody in New York who wanted to see it had? *The Man of La Mancha* had reruns until everybody saw it twice.

The most important thing the networks must do to promote the image of recycling is ask the government for money to make better use of its stockpile of old programs. A terrific start would have been to get taxpayers to finance a rerun of the 1968 Republican Presidential Convention last summer. Even President Nixon would have gone for that. Seeing John Lindsay nominating Spiro Agnew again would have won a lot of support for recycling.

Economic Indices. It's understandable that television industry leaders are gloomy about President Nixon's attempts to get the economy going again. The recession was a good thing for television.

When money is tight, people tend to spend less on entertainment. They stay at home more. Since most Americans have trouble communicating with each other, they tend to watch TV.

In hard times, all the shows' ratings go up across the board. So do the rates for commercials, based on the number of viewers per thousand. This in turn stimulates the economy of television executives in Westport, Conn. and Scarsdale, N. Y. Eventually it trickles down to the rest of the country.

In the old days, before the networks started relying on economic indices, they used to rely on the weather. Personally, I prefer the industry's former rationale for success or failure.

If a program did badly, it was common practice to check the Nielsens against the weather for that day. Low ratings were blamed on sunny skies. Conversely, exceptionally high ratings were credited to bad weather. Network officials were known to hope for cataclysmic weather to save shows. Floods were bad because they shortcircuited TV sets. Earthquakes were also bad for viewing. They made the pictures jiggle. But strong winds were fine.

Media buyers on Madison Avenue, I am told, used to consult *The Old Farmers' Almanac* before committing their clients to shows for the coming season. "Gray skies," on the day a special was scheduled would automatically get a sponsor. The networks, it is said, competed with each other in hiring groundhogs.

Economy Waves. While network presidents were assuring viewers that commercial television was healthier than ever, one sign of something wrong was the rash of firings at the three networks in 1971. The reason the papers gave was that profits were down during the recession.

That's true. A noted Wall Street brokerage house told investors that before-taxes profits at NBC plunged from $82 million in 1969 to $55 million in 1970. Although I'm not a trained accountant, it seems to me a corporation could be in a lot worse financial condition. It could actually be losing money.

I tried to find out when NBC last had a bad year (i.e., lost money). It hasn't had one of those yet. As Lord Thomson of Fleet once said: "A television license is a license to print money." With the business hitting what the networks call hard times— they were making money by the shovel load, instead of by the bucket load—the industry's leaders were panicking. Who got fired first but the news and public affairs people.

The networks have been throwing away the wheat and keeping the chaff. I've thought of a number of better areas where they could save money.

1. Stop editing movies for TV. Unedited movies would run longer, making it possible for the networks to buy fewer programs to run between the movies, a constant drain on network resources. Not only could the networks fire the film cutters, but also the huge broadcast standards and practices departments (censors) which dictate the cuts.

2. Fire the announcers who say, "We'll be back in a minute with the remainder of the program."

3. Let the vice presidents-in-charge-of-children's programming go. For years they've been flying out to the West Coast to arrange better programs for kids, with no apparent results.

4. Fire the networks' speechwriters. Anybody who can't write his own speech shouldn't be allowed to make one.

The really big money in economy waves is in firing the bosses, not the workers. *Business Week* reported recently that Dr. Frank Stanton's salary at CBS was $200,000. That's about what it costs to keep a complete news team (reporter, camera and sound men) in the field for a full year. Recessions are supposed to be hell.

Education of the Average Viewer.

It used to be said that, if it does not move, Jack Gould likes it. Nevertheless, the former *New York Times* television critic served an important function in the medium: his readers could be assured they would enjoy a show if he had panned it.

Unfortunately, the people who program educational television shows did not understand this simple fact as well as I did. For just as every magazine is edited with a Typical Reader in mind, so educational television had decided that its Average Viewer was Jack Gould.

Actually, Gould was above average. He usually liked serious programs, discussion shows and documentaries—provided they were socially relevant and gave "a balanced, fair treatment." If a show hinted there might indeed be only one answer to a problem, it was in critical trouble. He liked humor on television, but sometimes did not seem to have a sense of humor.

Gould was also very fond of opera on television. Perhaps he is an insomniac and opera is the only thing that can put him to sleep. Such are the secrets men carry around with them for years.

While all of this makes it sound as though I should be the Average Viewer for educational television programmers, I wouldn't be any better than Jack Gould. If I had my way, there would be nothing on the air but Pittsburgh Pirates' baseball games, adult movies, biting political satire—I agree with critic Stephanie Harrington that Mrs. John Mitchell should have her own telephone show—and mature soap operas. Power corrupts.

Electricity Consumption. Con Edison of
New York is currently running an advertising campaign, "Ten

Ways To Save A Watt." The eighth way states: "Turn off television sets . . . when you are not looking or listening."

This is tantamount to sabotage, since the structure of television is based on people leaving their sets on when they are not watching or listening to them. Many Nielsen families have been doing this for years. Actually, TV sets rank in the extreme bottom group of electricity-consuming devices, along with radios, little corner table lamps and electric clocks. It is just as logical for Con Edison to warn the public: "Turn off your electric clock when not reading the time."

TV should not be treated like just another appliance. It's degrading to be lumped together with dishwashers and air conditioners. TV is an art form, for God's sake.

If Con Edison was sincere about improving the quality of life, they would use a more moderate approach befitting a conservative monopoly: "Don't watch TV unless something good is on." But this only raises the problem of defining the word "good."

Elephants. In the opening ten minutes of an NBC documentary an elephant mother and her calf were photographed wandering around the African veldt looking for water. Cliff Robertson, the narrator in a helicopter who followed the wretched creature in her desperate search for eighty gallons of water, gave us the best play-by-play description of an elephant dying of thirst I've ever heard.

When the mother finally collapsed, my daughter asked, "Why did the elephant have to die?" For dramatic emphasis, I explained. It would have been a boring documentary without the death march. By letting the elephant mother die, the documentary seems to say that some elephants must die for their fellow elephants so that the public's attention can be called to their problem.

Had Robertson figured out a way to save that elephant, the

message of the documentary might have been that humans can do something to help the species. I wonder if it ever crossed the narrator's mind to use the helicopter to bring the mother elephant the eighty gallons of water.

The documentary might have been a little less powerful visually. But if a professed elephant-lover won't make sacrifices to help the breed, what can the rest of us be expected to do about it?

End of an Era. Two construction workers are eating lunch on the 110th floor of the World Trade Center, the largest skyscraper in the world, currently being built in downtown New York. A third walks by and falls off the edge.

"Hey, was that Harry?" asks one.

"Yup," says the other, looking down.

"Is he dead?"

"Yup."

The questioner takes a long drag on his cigarette and stares at it.

"Not half as dead as this cigarette," he says.

The above dialogue—created by Mark Schubin, a young amateur copywriter from New Jersey, as the finale for the long-playing Kools cigarette series of slice-of-life-as-it-really-isn't commercials—did not run the night of January 1, 1971. As a matter of fact, the cigarette advertisers didn't run any special commercials to mark that night, the night of their departure from television.

It's one of those things that cannot be dismissed lightly. I miss the commericals because they performed a valuable cultural function. Where else could we see such banal people, wandering through pleasant green fields and suddenly tearing off their clothes; being fascinated by packs of cigarettes which danced and sang; or caring about good taste or good grammar

58

in advertising, which usually gives us neither. The cigarette commercials were a better way to keep in touch with what was going on in America than the programs.

Not making anything of the demise is the last in a series of *faux pas* the cigarette industry made with its TV advertising since 1964, the start of all the talk about cigarettes being bad for the health. Since much of the talk came from scientists, I never understood why the industry didn't try to do something about that kind of bad publicity.

The cigarette commericals continued showing handsome young college football tackles kissing beauty queens. Subconsciously people were asking: Why are there only young folks in the commercials? Could it be that anybody who smoked that brand didn't live long enough to appear in the commercials?

Instead of the Marlboro Man, the image the industry should have striven for was the Old Man. I knew quite a few smokers back in the mid-1960s who would have accepted a fee to say something like, "I've smoked Camels for 25 years, and I'm still alive." But they weren't the right size, or didn't look good on camera.

Since the cigarette sponsors couldn't find anything good to say about the physical benefits of smoking cigarettes by the mid-1960s, I kept waiting for them to turn to the psychological benefits. "Uptight in social situations," a message along these lines might have run. "A cigarette at a party may be less harmful to your health than a shot of whisky." Those drunken driver commercials that the good-hands-people at All State Insurance Co. have been scaring us with this past holiday season also could have helped the tobacco industry.

By the late 1960s, everybody knew that cigarettes were dangerous. People who still smoked cigarettes probably had sound psychological reasons for continuing, such as a death wish. Still, the tobacco companies neglected to use TV to manipulate viewers with hard-hitting messages like "Brand X is harsher, faster-acting."

This sordid chapter in the history of advertising ingenuity

leads one to believe that the tobacco industry secretly would rather switch than fight. They were looking for an excuse to get out of TV. "What the ban on TV cigarette advertising really means," an executive at Brown & Williamson explained at the time, "is that we will be able to bank $20,000,000 in 1971." That viewers are such knee-jerk consumers that they run out to buy whatever they see advertised may be the biggest fallacy of the 20th Century.

Epidemics. Diseases are very contagious on TV. One of the most baffling cases in the annals of TV medicine was the outbreak several years back of Huntington's chorea, the disease that killed Woody Guthrie, the folk singer. It is extremely rare in real life. It seems there were more cases on TV at one time than in the whole United States, according to a recent study of epidemics made by the TV College of Medicine & Surgery. Huntington's chorea struck television shortly after *Alice's Restaurant*, starring Woody's son, Arlo, became a success at the box office.

This study of communicable disease (i.e., diseases which can be communicated by the broadcasting medium) isolates, for the first time, the pattern diseases take. After somebody on "Marcus Welby, M.D." comes down with, say, hydrophobia (rabies), it quickly spreads to the other networks' medical shows. Sometimes the pattern is reversed, with the disease hitting one of the other shows first and ending up at "Marcus Welby, M.D." Either way, it qualifies as an epidemic.

The symptoms in the plots are usually identical. First, the patient thinks he has the rare disease. Then it's found that he doesn't have it. That's the conflict.

The causes of the disease are well-known. Each disease has its followers. When it spreads to another medical show, it is thought that the viewers will come with it. So it's very difficult to stamp out the disease until it has run its course.

Eyewitness News. The basic format for television
news shows dates back to 1923, when Vladimir Zworkin invented the electronic scanner. The father of the modern TV set said, "Let there be a sixth and an eleventh hour news. And let there be anchorpeople reading the news in between the commercials. And let there be authorities on sports, movies and weather." And Zworkin rested.

Some historians believe all of this was actually said by Paul Nipkow, the German scientist who began experimenting with the transmission of pictures by wire in 1883.

I don't mean to imply that there aren't differences between the news shows. Of course there are, just as the Nassau County phone book is different from that of Suffolk or Westchester Counties.

News shows give you about twelve stories in thirty minutes. Even a dropout from the Evelyn Woods School can get the gist of the headlines and first paragraphs of at least three dozen stories in the same time by perusing a newspaper.

Walter Cronkite ends his CBS news show every night with the traditional "That's the way it is." Not everybody is convinced. For these reasons television news isn't my favorite source of information. But I continue watching it to keep tabs on the medium's foibles. The most amusing one I've noticed recently occurs at the end of "Eyewitness News" every night on WABC-TV (6 and 11 P.M.). It's the emerging art of "milling around."

This ritual begins immediately after the credits start to crawl across my TV set. The eyewitnesses who just moments ago were immobilized as they delivered the news suddenly begin walking around the studio.

When I first noticed it, the milling around seemed rather aimless. In recent months, as "Eyewitness News" has been growing in confidence with the rise of its ratings, the scene appears to be choreographed. The assorted newsmen, anchormen, sports-casters and weathermen—a cast of sixteen, not thousands—now seem to be milling around with a purpose. This is not easy. Try it.

The point to the milling around on "Eyewitness News," as explained by management, is that, "After the news, the newsmen just don't go their separate ways out the door for a beer. They talk to each other. It may come off as a little over-dramatized. But it would happen anyway. 'Eyewitness News' people really like each other."

The most widely publicized achievement of "Eyewitness News" is that Roger Grimsby likes Bill Beutel. They both like Melba Tolliver. That's why we should watch "Eyewitness News." The WABC-TV team sounds like either the Partridge Family of television journalism, or an encounter group.

Actually, Bill Beutel is a sensitive, intelligent fellow, and a pretty good newsman, and that's the real reason why you should watch "Eyewitness News." But saying something like that may be almost immoral in WABC-TV's approach to the news. Mentioning that somebody is a good newsman is liable to turn viewers off.

They also have a lot of private jokes on "Eyewitness News" that break up everybody in the studio. The viewer doesn't know what's so funny. While this gives the show the flavor of a cocktail party a stranger has wandered into, it is not good journalism. Still, someday "Eyewitness News" should win a prize for honesty. Everybody in the business knows there's more to TV news than information: it's part-journalism and part-show business. It takes courage to openly demonstrate this on the air.

The FCC Hearings on CATV in 1970. *Broadcasting* magazine said the hearings affected the evolution of cable television as much as the evolution of the monkey was affected by the Barnum & Bailey Circus.

Fear of Offending. The invention of the fear of offending by smell is considered, in some circles, the foremost contribution of the American people to civilization. It was long known that humans smelled, but it took the genius of Madison Avenue to realize that people smelled bad.

Great Britain was, perhaps, the last country in the western

world to discover this truth. That may be due to the almost twenty-year delay between the invention of British television (circa 1936) and the inception of interrupting programs with commercials (1955). "The only reason they didn't have commercials for so long is that they didn't think of it first," Robert Morley once said. "Pride is a very important matter in Britain."

The showing of commercials on the British Independent Television Network (ITV) performed a useful function at first. "Thanks to the BBC, the people didn't know what to buy when they went into the stores," an American living in Cambridge says. "It was terrible to see them wandering aimlessly in the aisles. They hadn't the slightest idea what Prince Philip or David Frost favored. It was pathetic."

ITV soon told them. In fact, British ad agencies have been so successful in making their people smell-conscious and afraid of offending, you can't even smell brussel sprouts in the halls of the finest hotels any more. "If you do smell them, it comes from cans of aerosol spray," British TV critic Elkan Allan says. "We know you Americans want that odor. It's what you consider typically English. We're a lot smarter than you think."

"Firing Line." On "Firing Line" Bill Buckley throws open the floor to questions from college students in the audience for ten minutes at the end of each debate. That's like Joe Frazier offering to fight any guy in the house. Anybody who could out-talk Bill Buckley would have his own show on public TV. The liberals lose so consistently on "Firing Line" that the show should be called "Firing Squad."

The First Amendment in Baseball.
People don't seem to go to the ballpark to watch the games anymore. They go to wave to the television cameras. TV reporting contributes to this phenomenon by regularly focusing on the

crowd action in lieu of more substantial investigation of the base-ball action. Anyway, it's a lot more exciting watching the spec-tators in the stands than hearing all that statistical prattle.

Some fans come to the stadium and start fights every Friday night just to get on TV. Others write signs. A few seasons back, I recommended that television cater to this normal instinct by putting the crowd scenes on a set schedule: the third-base crowd after the second inning, the people behind first base after the fourth inning, and so on. Then they would know what was coming. You wouldn't find them picking their noses or not show-ing the camera their best side. The parks would be filled every night. A pretty blonde in the bleachers could become a movie starlet after being spotted on TV by an alert casting director. Baseball telecasts would be the electronic equivalent of Schwab's Drugstore in Hollywood.

But now censorship in baseball-fan reporting has reared its ugly head. The first instance of censorship I discovered while watching the New York Mets [WOR-TV] took place during the third or fourth inning of a Friday night game in 1971 with the Pittsburgh Pirates. Met pitcher Charley Williams was at bat, the count was 3–2, and the cameras were roaming the stands looking for a big story. A young fellow on the third-base side, noticing the cameras were on him, placed his hand on the breast of the girl in the next seat. (Well, not everybody can write a great sign.) I couldn't tell whether it was his date or an innocent bystander. The cameras immediately zoomed out to center field, missing Charley Williams' dramatic strike-out in their excite-ment. The same thing happened later that night whenever fans crossed their arms in irritation at some turn of the game or gave the TV men the finger.

Several nights afterward, the cameras were covering a pep rally in the stands during the Mets–Cubs game. Viewers at home could hear the chant from the youngsters: *Fuck YOU, New York Mets, Fuck YOU*. But not for long. The sound equipment broke down, or something. Technical difficulties also cropped up when the fans were yelling, *Ferguson Jenkins Eats Shit*.

65

As the weeks went by, I began to notice a pattern. Anytime the spectators said something the station considered in questionable taste, the TV screen immediately stopped registering what was happening in the stands. Baseball had become a director's game!

I suppose the station could justify its policy. Yet how do we know that "Atlanta Sucks," another phrase heard for a fleeting moment, isn't some kind of obscure baseball term which, under the Supreme Court ruling, is not obscene? The classic baseball expression, "We want a hit"—allowed on the air without thought of censorship—could be interpreted in different ways, too. The fans could be ordering the assassination of a rival pitcher or making a general appeal for drugs.

I went to the New York Civil Liberties Union (NYCLU) for guidance on this confusing matter of free speech. Ira Glasser, the executive director and ex-Brooklyn Dodger fan, explained: "Apparently it was okay in the old days of radio for Red Barber to use mysterious expressions like 'tearing up the pea patch.' Today that sounds suspicious, with the media's overcautious attitude to words. God knows what Preacher Roe was doing when Barber said he had 'one foot in the pickle fat.'"

Glasser and Alan Levine, the NYCLU counsel, believe a good case could be made for fans who feel their civil liberties are being encroached upon by the station's editing out their remarks. Freedom of speech, my legal advisers asserted, signifies more than the right to talk in a dark corner. It implies the right to be audible. In the eighteenth century, leafleting was the way to be heard. Today it is through TV. "Without the medium," Levine said, "there is no message. The kids have to do something out of the ordinary to be heard by the medium. The burning of draft cards is a way to get TV to cover their opposition to the war. Protesters are learning to make their protest more visual."

One solution for TV baseball would be to seal off the ballfields with glass, in the style of the isolation booths of the '50s quiz shows. If all baseball games were played in a TV studio, crowd noises could be artificially produced, like the laugh tracks on situation comedies.

66

"The Following Program is Brought to You as a Public Service." This means
that the station couldn't find a sponsor for it. Often used in connection with documentaries and news.

Forest Fires. When the economy is down, TV fans see
a lot of anti-pollution and anti-forest fire commercials. Not that there's anything wrong with anti-forest fire commercials. There hasn't been a single forest fire in New York City since they began running.

Friday Night at the Movies. See: "Monday Night at the Movies".

Frost, David. Are the people who get their information from TV more misinformed than people who get their information from newspapers? A good case can be made for both groups being tied for dead last in the race to know what's going on in the government. But I think TV is doing a much better job of misinforming.

What other medium, for example, would entrust the interviewing of the vice president of the United States for ninety minutes to a former satirist like David Frost (a highlight of the 1971 talk-show civics lessons)? The vice president could have told Frost that we have never bombed Vietnam, and Frost would have said "marvelous."

And Frost is a well-informed Englishman compared to Joey Bishop on the sociological implications of drugs, Johnny Carson

67

on the population explosion, David Susskind on anything, or Hugh Downs on menopause ("It is," he once said on NBC's "Today," "a controversial subject.").

Gamma Rays.

The government's triumphant announcement that they have finally compelled television set manufacturers to reduce the X-rays emanating from our TV sets to the point where they are no longer considered dangerous has alarmed the hell out of me. By reducing the X-rays, are our sets now producing more gamma rays?

As a matter of fact, when was the last time anybody checked our 80,000,000 sets for gamma rays (which scientists describe as "very high energy X-rays")? Gamma rays are emitted by decaying radioactive substances, and there's a high percentage of dead material on our TV sets.

The entertainment programs this season are making a lot of us nauseous. Documentaries and discussion shows make us listless. The commericals leave us irritable and jumpy. Late-night talk shows give many women a headache when they go to bed. Perhaps these physical by-products of watching television have nothing to do with the programs, as it has always been assumed.

The networks should be pouring millions into studies by research laboratories to investigate what the sets, rather than the programs, do to us.

We may be mutating at this very moment. Have our stomachs grown larger since the Electronic Age began, and our mental capacity smaller? Many of us, for example, have already forgotten how to read. Perhaps the next change will be bigger eyeballs—the size of cantaloupes, Fred Allen once predicted, to go with brains the size of peas. And then smaller ears. Do we have to start growing little antennas before the government becomes concerned about TV's impact on viewers?

Ralph Nader ought to urge the television industry to recall the nation's 80,000,000 TV sets until they have been properly tested. And maybe while the sets are in the laboratories, the networks will have the time to think about the programs.

Gifford and Rote. The TV sports world was
shaken when CBS's ace sportscaster Frank Gifford went to ABC. The report is that he was traded for two left-handed film editors from the Pacific Coast affiliate, a wall-eyed cameraman and three union technicians whose only qualification is their ability to say, "It can't be done."

It was shaken once again when NBC announced that Kyle Rote was retiring to make room for a rookie announcer, Dick Schaap, the literary man. Still, Rote's talking days were not over. He went to CBS.

All of this moving around of Gifford and Rote is upsetting. It comes at a time when I had finally got straight in my mind who they were. One of the most controversial subjects in the sports field for the past five years has been how viewers tell the difference between Gifford and Rote.

Gifford is more handsome than Rote, although both are good-looking. Gifford wears his hair differently than Rote. Neither Rote nor Gifford moves his eyes when reading the sport news. They have a special teleprompter, I've been told, which has one word printed on a line so we won't see the eyeballs moving. It's supposed to look more natural that way, although it probably gives a fellow stiff eyeballs. Both Rote and Gifford never move their lips when they speak.

The method that finally worked for me is remembering that Gifford is the one who could be seen in the kitchen on the Westinghouse commericals. If there's a handsome sportscaster standing around an electric range or refrigerators, not moving his lips, you can be sure it's Gifford.

Jim Bouton of WABC-TV chewed me out. "It's not that hard," Bouton explained at the annual City College Editor & Publisher banquet. "Kyle is the one who says Detroit beat Minnesota. Frank is the one who says Detroit *over* Minnesota. You fool!"

Green Rooms. Whenever I have nothing better to do, I like to stop by the Green Room at one of the major talk shows and listen to the guests chew the fat. Often the comments they make off camera are more entertaining and revealing than what they say on camera.

The Green Room, for any of you who still haven't been invited to be a guest on a talk show, is a small room adjacent to the stage and usually contains from six to twelve theories about why it's called the Green Room. Some say it's because the room contributes to the guests' anxiety, envy, or nausea.

Anyway, most guests think of it as the Blue Room. It's a very depressing place. They are locked in there by the producers a few minutes before the taping is scheduled to begin. For some guests, it is the only time they ever watch talk shows. If the person on the screen they are being forced to watch is terrific, that doesn't make the captive audience very happy. It's a tough act to follow. If the guest on the stage is bombing, that doesn't trigger whistling or cheering either. It means that the show is being turned off all over the country. The audience at home won't even get to see the guy who has been waiting in the Green Room for as long as one hour and fifty-five minutes.

The Green Room has the same fascination for a TV critic that the gallows used to have for crime reporters.

Handelman, Stanley Myron. The problem with news analysts today, Handelman explained, is that they are always looking backward. The new direction for news analysis should be forward. Stanley Myron Handelman someday would like to become the nation's first TV news forecaster.

"I would tell the people what's coming in the near future so they can plan their life accordingly. Instead of the word COMMENT under my picture on the screen, there should be the word REPENT. Most analysts base their interpretations of the news on hope. My interpretations would be based on how much time is left, so people can start repenting faster."

Off the top of his head, Handelman gave me a sample of a typical day's news forecasting:

"My think piece about pollution. If we spent a million dollars a day cleaning up the air—I think that's less than what we spend on the Vietnam war—I'd tell the people it's not enough to stop pollution. It would just be a matter of time until we all choke. A good forecaster should be able to figure out just how much time is left.

"What does the stock market drop mean? I'd look ahead and predict a consolidation of money in the hands of the rich. Very little money will remain in the hands of the poor. There should be a massive federal campaign to re-educate the people on the merits of poverty. They might come up with a new slogan, like 'The meek shall inherit the earth.' The kids could learn it easier if it was written into the Pledge of Allegiance.

"I know this must sound as depressing as hell," Handelman said, pulling his cap further down on his head. "But my natural wit will take the sting out of my forecasts."

Hearings. Channel 13 in New York performed an important public service by giving us seventeen hours and forty-one minutes of the India–Pakistan crisis at the U.N. Without the live coverage and taped highlights, we wouldn't have known that the machinery for settling international disputes doesn't work.

The drama in the U.N. coverage was like one of those plays David Susskind and his Talent Ltd. are famous for on TV: a lot of talk and little action. The U.N. coverage was exceptionally boring and exceptionally valuable—a combination which pretty much describes what public service on TV is all about.

As entertainment, however, the U.N. coverage did not measure up to the Knapp Commission hearings—Channel 13's fifty-nine-hour-and-twenty-seven-minute-long examination of the way the police code of ethics doesn't work. That study of the great old American institution of police corruption had drama as well as some of the finest singing heard on TV that year. The police establishment denounced these hearings as "a circus." I disagree. They were by far the best detective story of the season.

The New York State Legislature show—the third in Channel 13's continuing examination of processes that don't work very well—also fell below the entertainment standards set by the Knapp Commission. The script for Act I wasn't nearly as tight, the cast of characters not so perfect. But I have high hopes for this continuing drama about a state and its financial problems.

As far as is known, this was the first time the legislature had been televised in action. Either because of inexperience with the medium, or by design, the legislators were two-and-a-half hours late in raising the curtain the first day. The gavel was finally banged, and the first order of business was to adjourn. Every time the cast of characters assembled that first week, it seemed to be to adjourn. Maybe the strategy was to make the session so boring that Channel 13 would go away.

The History of the Nude in TV.
Between 1945 and 1972, NBC twice showed nudes on serious drama programs. Of course, they were only naked from the waist up, and they were men. But it was a step in the right direction.

Hitler, Adolf. A TV documentary about Hitler would
try to be fair to both sides, treating the victims and their oppressors as if they were equal.

Holding Up the Book.

I've become a little uptight about the extreme measures revolutionaries of the Hoffman stripe are taking to destroy the electronic media. Hoffman, I learned the other day, is a new member of the American Federation of Television and Radio Artists (AFTRA), one of the more wealthy and conservative unions. Before appearing on WNET's "Newsfront" (1970)—a golden opportunity to radicalize millions of moderate TV viewers—he insisted on a $100 honorarium.

I haven't asked Abbie why he joined the forces of reaction at AFTRA. But I assume one reason is that Merv Griffin requires you to be a card-carrying member to talk on his CBS program.

In the First Amendment furor over the way CBS handled Hoffman's choice of clothing for the evening of March 28, 1970, it is easy to forget the fact that he went on "The Merv Griffin Show" to plug his book. So much has been said about the stupidity of the CBS decision to black out—actually, on color sets it was a blue-out—Hoffman and his flag shirt. It reminded me of the Kremlin's painting Beria out of pictures after the purge, as if his crimes would then cease to exist.

This instance of electronic cowardice cheated viewers of the chance to see Hoffman, the revolutionary, shilling his book like any other doctrinaire capitalist writer. Somebody who was at the show that night recalled that Hoffman held up the book, attacked his publisher for changing a few lines of type and, for the *coup de grace,* threw the book at Griffin.

Carrying around one's book to television shows ranks high among the more humiliating aspects of writing these days. When the producers of "Newsfront" were trying to set up their debate, Jerry Rubin reportedly listed as one of his non-negotiable demands that a copy of his new book be held up by the host. Mitchell Krauss refused. Rubin showed up for the taping with ten copies of his book anyway—an example of the excesses of revolutionary fervor.

The debate ended with the Rubin–Hoffman–Davis team clearly outpointing Wechsler–Rovere–Dorsen by alternately ridiculing, bullying, ignoring, and nonsequituring their elders. After it was all over, and the winners were eating hamburgers provided by the Eastern Educational Network, Rubin took Krauss aside. The revolutionary had verbally assaulted and physically pushed the moderator on the air. "How did we do?" Rubin asked his vanquished host.

"You were great," Krauss assured the revolutionary hero.

Holy Cows.

A lot of fans walk around with the fantasy that they could do a better job broadcasting baseball games than the talented fellows currently doing it. Woody Allen got the chance to show his stuff for one inning of a New York Yankee game in July, 1967, and no longer has any illusions.

"It was either the fourth or fifth," Woody recalled in New York on the set of *Bananas* (1970), the first motion picture he ever directed. "It was on either radio or TV. They didn't tell me."

It was radio. The management of the New York Yankees had promised the actor-comedian a shot at doing a TV broadcast, too. As far as the Yankees were concerned, it was just another publicity stunt (to plug a charity softball game, which Mayor Lindsay was promoting and Allen was to play in, to aid the city's parks). But for Allen it meant a chance to sit in the hallowed seat of such a sports broadcasting personality as Phil Rizzuto.

"It was a lot harder than I thought," Allen said of the experience of being "the 10th Yankee." "The first man I called hit a ball down to first. I said that, but it sounded terribly dull. You have to get a sense of urgency in your voice. It's a real form of acting: you have to give the play motivation. I knew I wouldn't be any good at baseball; it was unnatural for me."

Seeing their new colleague floundering around, the regulars in the Yankee booth—Rizzuto and Joe Garagiola, now a star on NBC's "Today Show"—handed him some statistics to pep up his play-by-play. The Yankees of 1967 were a terrible team.

Allen tried reading the averages of all the players hitting under .200. "No wonder they're doing so badly," Allen explained.

Bobby Richardson, the Yankees' star infielder, stepped into the batter's box. Instead of saying that while Bobby was hitting only .167, he looked good the last few times he hit the ball hard right back to the pitcher—Allen observed that he was surprised that a major leaguer should be such a poor hitter. "When I was a player," Allen said, drawing, in the traditional manner, on his background as an ex-athlete, "I had tremendous power—to all fields."

A "holy cow!" cut through the silence in the broadcasting booth· Allen guessed Phil Rizzuto was commenting on his style.

The Yankees were losing that day, and Allen took a stab at analysis. "Well, of course, the guys on the other team don't stay out as late at night as our guys. Look at Jake Gibbs (the Yankee catcher coming to bat). I'm in better shape than he is."

Another "holy cow!" split the air. "I thought I said something wrong," Allen recalls. He decided to change his tack.

The novice broadcaster began a short lecture to the kids listening to the game praising the Yankees. "Loose living and going to nightclubs is the only way for a ballplayer to stay in shape," he said.

"Late hours and bad food," Allen's homilies continued, "are the key to making you become a good hitter. If you want to be a great fielder, drop out of school and play ball all the time.

"I was in the midst of knocking some ballplayer for hitting a hard line drive that just went foul and then missing the third strike completely. Garagiola sensed that I was in trouble and he came to my defense."

"What most people at home don't understand," Garagiola said, "is that a guy can be hitting a ball well and have bad luck. A couple of feet can mean the difference between a .300 hitter and a .260 hitter."

"But this guy is hitting .240," Allen argued. "No wonder we're in fourth place."

Woody Allen was benched after one half of his inning was

over. "Holy cow!" he heard Phil Rizzuto tell the radio audience in a critique as he left sadly for the showers. "What was that all about?" It was a new high in criticism for the former Yankee shortstop.

"There was nothing controversial about what I said," Woody explained in a post-game interview three years later. "No ideas were expresed that could not have been uttered on 'The Ed Sullivan Show.' But Rizzuto and the Yankee organization were outraged. When I tried to find out what I had done wrong, everybody said I wasn't showing respect for the kids who love baseball. But the major league ball club managements don't show respect either. After using the media to seduce kids into becoming loyal fans, they pull the franchises and leave."

Woody Allen's debut as a TV broadcaster was canceled in the wake of his having a little innocent fun on the radio. If only he would make a comeback as a baseball announcer. The broadcasting game needs men like him.

Ideas for New TV Series:

1) The Tree Surgeons
2) The Bookkeepers
3) The Roto Rooter Men

Incursion.

When Napoleon returned from exile at Elba, the first French newspaper headlines read, "The Beast Lands at Marseilles." A few days later they reported, "Bonaparte in Lyons." As he entered the capital, while King Louis XVIII was fleeing, the papers said: "His Excellency, the Honorable Napoleon, in Paris."

Language changes with the passing of events. Still, I am sorry to see that word "incursion" has gone into decline on the television news shows, even though most viewers never quite understood what it meant. It added a lot of class to the average TV news program script, never known for its erudition.

There's a long tradition of Americans being baffled by what's going on in Asia. On a Mississippi TV press conference show a few years back, a reporter asked Governor Ross Barnett, then up for re-election: "What about Quemoy and Matsu?"

The governor replied, "I'll find a place for them on the Fish and Game Commission."

During the last few weeks of the Laos Incursion newscasters deserted the word like rats leaving a sinking ship. They began using pseudo-words like "action," "operation," and "drive" to describe what was clearly an "incursion." When the retreat of the South Vietnamese troops reached its peak, TRB in *The New Republic* even used the phrase "Laos Excursion." Nobody on the television news shows went that far.

An administration's motive in using a new word is sound: by calling something something else a problem is liable to go away. The creative use of language solved the Negro problem on television. Today we never hear about the Negro problem any more, although newscasters still mention a black problem.

Nobody ever questions why the *New York Times* one day—I believe it was in 1937—suddenly started using the word "insurgents" instead of "rebels" as a noun for General Franco's revolting army. But our administration is ridiculed in television news circles for trying to improve our vocabulary with "incursion." One news executive even suggested that a memorandum is circulated in Washington saying, "The obscure word for the week is . . ."

Even worse, many neutral television viewers assume the administration made up the word "incursion." How short human memory is!

I began looking into the origin of the word the first time it was mentioned on a news show—but I embargoed publication of my research, lest it hurt whatever-it-was that was happening in Laos—and found that the word went farther back than President Nixon. Actually "incursion" is an old Indochinese word.

Visitors to the ancient temple of Angkor Wat, in the jungles of Cambodia, have seen honorable word "incursion" written over the entrance. It means "penetration." Visitors to the ruins, which date back to 1100, have also seen another old Indochinese word on the back door, "withdrawal." This comes from the old Roman *war interruptus.*

Some linguistic authorities claim these words are actually sexual terms, and thus in bad taste for use on the six o'clock news, but acceptable for the eleven o'clock news. That's one argument I don't want to get involved in.

Having promised us no more invasions in Indochina, the word is that the administration is pouring through the thesaurus looking for a new way to explain what went on. I think they should have called it the "Laos Evasion."

Interruptions. The NBC peacock, which had been on

the air probably as often as Hugh Downs, was limited to only three appearances a day in 1971–72. The NBC animated chime logo, promos, credit crawls and other interruptions were either eliminated or drastically cut back, adding as much as thirty seconds per program. The implication behind the NBC purge of the clutter area was that there is something wrong with the interruptions on TV. I was wondering who told NBC, after all these years, that interruptions were distracting?

(We'll be back with The Marvin Kitman TV Show in a moment. But first a few words about what's next in Marvin Kitman's TV Guide. It's terrific. And now back to the Marvin Kitman TV Guide.)

The interruption is one of the medium's oldest traditions. As a matter of record, there are more interruptions than programs on television every day.

(This is page 80 of The Marvin Kitman TV Show. Be sure to read letter "C" right away. Don't miss the expose of the secret CIA plot to undermine the Cuban economy by unloading U.S. government surplus saccharine, wrecking the world sugar market.)

It's such an old custom, viewers often forget what is being interrupted. By now they just assume the steady stream of interruptions has something to do with the FCC licenses. And if it doesn't, it should.

(More to come on "Interruptions." This is still The Marvin Kitman TV Show.)

Some respected critics even say that interruptions and clutter are what television is all about. Eliminating them would be a case of throwing away the wheat and keeping the chaff, or the programs.

(The ninth paragraph of the Marvin Kitman's "Interruptions" is just a few paragraphs away. It's really a good one. We now return you to the discussion in progress.)

(But first this message. The illustrations elsewhere in this Encyclopedic Show are also worth looking at.)

The interruptions are the bulwark of the American system of broadcasting. Without them, unemployment on Madison Avenue would rise. The consumption of snacks would drop. Commerical television would be just like public broadcasting.

(It's 8:30 in the morning as The Marvin Kitman TV Show is being written. It's time for a brief break to remind you that this is the local edition of Marvin Kitman's TV Guide.)

Clutter serves an important function in the medium. The print medium has logical built-in pauses, the end of sentences, paragraphs, pages and chapters. But television also has an inherent logic. It divides a movie, for example, into equal parts: 12 (minutes), 12, 12, 10, 10, 8, 8, 4, 4, 2, 2, 2.

(Have you noticed the typeface on this page? The best typeface in this edition of the Guide. Now stay right where you are for the final paragraphs of the "Interruptions" entry in The Marvin Kitman TV Show.)

The interruptions are also important on the intellectual ghetto discussion shows. William F. Buckley said the other day the lack of pauses on public broadcasting may hurt the intellectual stature of his new debate show. "Once you're on the wrong track," he said, explaining why he preferred his old commercial broadcasting show, "you continue to be on the wrong track. The pauses gave you time to collect your thoughts."

(The "Interruptions" entry in The Marvin Kitman TV Show was based on an original idea by General Sarnoff and was written on an Underwood standard typewriter, on white paper.)

The worst thing about reducing the interruptions like the NBC peacock and the NBC animated chime logo is that it creates an identity crisis. If CBS and ABC followed suit, how would viewers know which network's programs they were watching?

(Paper courtesy of Newsday and Outerbridge & Lazard. Additional ideas and coffee supplied by Carol Kitman. Typographical errors courtesy of typesetter.)

Removing thirty seconds of clutter next season is definitely a step in the wrong direction. It only reminds viewers of all the interruptions still remaining on the networks.

ITT. See "Morton's Lemon Cream Pie."

"I've Got a Secret." Nobody thinks there's anything wrong with the publication of secrets about the Civil War,

such as the fact that President Grant drank while on active duty. The reason we accept that bad news is that the secret came out slowly in history books.

These days, some reporter stumbles on a secret like the My Lai massacre or the Pentagon papers and suddenly everybody knows about it. The best thing the administration has thought of to slow down the process is the court injunction proceeding.

A better way to drain all the drama and excitement out of the process, it seems to me, is to let our secrets come out on a television game show. My plan for making a more relevant version of "I've Got a Secret" works like this:

Each week alumni from previous administrations will be invited on the show to present a secret from one of his old Defense Department or State Department files that has been gathering dust at home. These secrets will be more interesting than the secrets they used to have on the original version of "I've Got a Secret," like "I played the kazoo with the New York Philharmonic when nobody was listening." While viewers are mulling over the secret—trying to make up their own minds about whether it is truly a classified document or only one that has been classified by mistake—the former government official contestant will be grilled by the panel of jurists:

"Is your secret current or past?"

"Does your secret jeopardize national security or only the reputations of your former employers?"

"Will the publication of your secret prolong or shorten the war?"

"Do greater or fewer than 100 people have copies of your secret?"

A variation on this format will have three or four former government officials presenting the same secret. The game ends with the host asking, "Will the real informer stand up?"

Further details about the show are classified. But I can reveal that the panelist on the blue-ribbon jury of federal judges who guesses the real secret wins a prize: a free trip to the FBI building in Washington, where he get a chance to see his dossier. The contestant who presented a real secret wins a free trip to beautiful downtown Fort Leavenworth, Kansas.

Kitman's Law. On the TV screen, pure drivel tends to drive off ordinary drivel.

Krassner vs. Wallace on Censorship.
"What about all those four-letter words in your magazine?" Mike Wallace of CBS once asked a young radical magazine editor, on the air. "Which ones do you mean, Mike?" answered Paul Krassner of *The Realist*.

An example of self-censorship at its finest, with both sides pitching in to help each other shut up.

Lingeman Foundation.

A reliably informed source told me recently the government is exploring the principle of protecting its secrets by overexposing them. The secret government study prepared by the Richard Lingeman Foundation in 1963, is code-named "Open Files Plan."

The government is spending millions to protect classified information, the Lingeman study found. "They spend it for safes, locks, filing cabinets, barbed wire fences, guards, background investigations, the FBI, CIA, ASA, CIC and freelance spies. Despite this vast apparatus, we know that reporters are constantly penetrating our security system and stealing our secrets.

"The Open Files Plan solves the security problem by eliminating it—and saves the American taxpayer millions of dollars in the bargain.

"Under the Open Files Plan," the secret study continues, "all classified information would be declassified and our files thrown open to journalists. The beauty of this plan is that it would thoroughly confuse the enemy. No longer will the government help the reporters do their jobs by stamping 'Top Secret' on the most important information.

"Thousands of man-hours would be consumed in wading

through mountains of dull government documents looking for a secret. Publishers wouldn't stand for that kind of wasted money.

"Even when a reporter does find a secret," the Lingeman report explains, "he can't be sure it really *is* a secret. Thus he would be haggling constantly with his editors over whether the text of some massive document was worth reprinting.

"Of course, all those reporters running around government offices and digging through the files would cause congestion," the Lingeman report concludes, "so eventually it might be wise to put all the government documents—the memoranda, mash notes, expense accounts, every piece of government paper—in one large clearing house, called a Public Information Office, or Spy Library.

"The Spy Library would be open to all journalists who could prove a sincere interest in embarrassing the government. Reporting would become a tedious, low-paying job, stripped of all its cloak-and-dagger glamor, and newspapers would have as much trouble hiring good reporters as *Time* magazine has finding competent researchers."

Alarmed by the drop in interest in its secrets, my informed source explained, the government would next try to provide maximum exposure by putting all its papers on micro video-tape and play its secrets on one of those open channels on cable television twenty-four hours a day, like a Congressional Record of the air. "It will save the reporters the trouble of having to go to the library," my source explained.

Live Audiences.
In the bad old days of canned laughter, situation-comedy producers wouldn't dare start the laugh track as soon as the star came into focus. They had to wait until the star said something, like "Hi, honey" (titters). "I'm home for dinner" (chuckles). "You mean this is Wednesday, not Tuesday, and my boss is *not* coming for dinner tonight?" (guffaws).

To everybody's amazement the new live audiences which were supposed to eliminate that kind of abuse have turned out to be worse than the laugh track.

All of which is giving "live audiences" a bad name. But before we write them off, it should be asked where television gets those people? From Los Angeles.

The people in California are well-known for being generally more responsive to everything—the latest fad, the latest religion, the latest TV shows. A kind of gallows humor is prevalent out there. The people feel the sword over their head, what with living so close to the San Andreas Fault, the smog, and their homes in constant danger of being washed off the hills. If President Nixon were defeated, he would probably come back to live in California. Any number of disasters await them, so it's no wonder that when they come out of their homes to see the latest TV situation comedy, they fill the studios with laughter.

"Not all of it is laughter," explained Dr. Harvey Jacobs, an authority. "I would estimate that only about twenty percent of the audience in the average sitcom studio are inveterate guffawers. A lot of the laughing is actually repressed coughing. When they leave the studio, eighty percent of the Los Angeles studio audience goes into an immediate depression."

My own feeling is that situation comedies today—like "All in the Family," "The Odd Couple," "The Mary Tyler Moore Show," "Sanford and Son"—are becoming so amusing in themselves that TV no longer needs audiences laughing as a guide to what's funny. It needs canned silence.

Unfortunately, canned silence would be anathema to TV, with its high standards for honesty.

"The way to have both live audiences and silence," Jacobs suggested, "is taping the shows in a Trappist monastery."

M. The letter "M" is brought to you by the Ford Foundation. If they had given me some Money to compile this encyclopedia, it would still be unfinished. I would like to acknowledge my debt to the Ford people for not underwriting this project, one of the few major events in broadcasting it hasn't sponsored. But I still think Ford would better serve society by putting its money into basic research, such as developing an automobile that would last as long as the 1948 models.

Maimonides. Maimonides, the twelfth century physician and philosopher, lists about 600 laws by which people should govern themselves, none of which seem to be followed too closely these days.

The first law of giving, according to Maimonides, is that the donor should not be publicly known. The highest form of charity requires that the donor be unknown even to the recipient—lest the recipient be overly humble in his future dealings with the man.

The most popular form of charity in televisionland is the grant. Maimonides didn't anticipate the special problems of the large charitable and corporate foundations. An interesting case in point occurred recently when the Mobil Oil Corporation, one of the largest industrial firms of the nation, called a press conference at Toots Shor's Restaurant to announce they were giving a sum to public broadcasting "in excess of $1,000,000."

At Toots Shor's, it was explained that the million dollars would be spent in the following two ways: $490,000 for "Masterpiece Theater," a series of thirty-nine original one-hour dramas produced by BBC, and $250,000 for copies of the *Sesame Street Magazine* to be given away free to disadvantaged school children.

It is not nice to look a gift horse in the mouth, but the press asked what the other $260,000 was for. In effect, the money was to be used to publicize the corporation's contribution to television culture.

The "Mammy." See "Crass Commercialism."

A Man's World. In 1970, NBC presented a TV special entitled "A Man's World," a study of twentieth century man, hosted by Hugh O'Brian. In his examination of what is happening in the world of men today, O'Brian chose to look at the life styles of Phil Collins, composer-dramatist-singer and a leading member of the Flaming Youth rock group in London; Michael "Turk" Turkington, a surfer who lives in a Volkswagen van in Hawaii; Jean Bouquin, who designs unusual men's clothes to order in Paris, while himself dressing like a first-class slob; Eduardo "Lalo" Azcue, a millionaire lawyer in Mexico City who lives for the weekend when he plays with his jet-set friends in Acapulco; and Om-Dish-A-Daer, a Berber tribesman who works as an acrobat in Marrakech. That's what I call a real cross-section of men.

Some male viewers may have felt vaguely uneasy about a portrait which sums up the man's world today in terms of writing and singing flat lyrics in Soho, looking for "a perfect wave" in Hawaii, sewing clothes in Paris and spearing a bull in the eye in Acapulco and hissing, "Bull, you are going to die." Obviously nobody would want to watch a special about the life styles of, say, a television critic, a mailman or a discount store executive— as exciting as they may be.

But I don't mind confessing that I found myself wondering about what is manly. Three of O'Brian's specimens have long hair. (Mine is curly and wearing it long makes me look like Shirley Temple.) No matter how I try, I can't become interested in sewing or designing clothes. Surfing makes me seasick. And that Arab was really obsessed with courage.

NBC could have lessened the anxiety feelings it raised in the television audience by calling its documentary "A Man's Fantasy World." Not that O'Brian's study could be said to be everyman's fantasy world.

Freud said it was good to talk out fantasies. So this *Boy's Life* view of man may have been a useful hour. "I really dig chicks that are quiet," Turk the surfer explained about his dream girl. Sure he does: the other kind might want to know when he was going to get a job. O'Brian tried to make the courturier Bouquin's life glamorous in Paris, but it still looked like a sweatshop in the garment center to me. As thrilling as the fantasy of becoming an Arab acrobat may be, what happens to his instincts after he hits thirty?

Smoking pot on the road to Marrakech, whiling away the months at parties in Acapulco, pleasure and thrill seeking are the fantasies of seventeen-year-olds. The least "A Man's World" could have done was include a token man who is committed to improving the world. Some men still have fantasies about becoming president of U.S. Steel. "They are marching to different drummers," as Hugh O'Brian said, quoting what Henry Thoreau said.

Marcus Welby, M.D. I watch "Marcus Welby,

M.D." for the acting. But a lot of Americans watch this ABC show as a kind of documentary on the medical profession. They must have been shocked recently when a patient actually paid Doc Welby for services rendered. Even if it was only an apple pie.

"This raises a conflict-of-interest problem," explained an ABC executive who couldn't remember the sordid subject of fees ever being raised before on the popular medical show. "He usually works for the good of it. But don't worry: we're going to look into this. There'll probably be a flood of protest mail from the AMA, and we want to be prepared."

"Marcus Welby, M.D.," in this way, seems to be an unpaid advertisement for socialized medicine, slipped into the dramas every week by the Communists and liberals who, readers tell me, control the networks. Patients go to Doc Welby's office and are treated week after week regardless of race, creed, previous condition of their bank accounts or credit ratings. And Doc Welby isn't the only TV doctor practicing socialism. In the history of TV medicine, there has never been a doctor who has been shown charging a patient a dime for some of the best medical attention the world has ever seen.

Obviously this can't be true. It's against all the principles that Doc Welby and the TV medical profession stand for.

Judging by the standard of living depicted on the show, Doc Welby seems to live very well. The money has to come from somewhere. It's always possible he has another business on the side, like a gas station, that can support his altruism at the office.

I prefer to think that he's charging the patients, but the show just doesn't have time to get into that aspect of the profession.

Surmising his rates, takes some calculation: A successful doctor of Robert Young's stature in the profession earns roughly $100,000 for a fifty-two-week year. But Doc Welby works only twenty-six weeks a year, only one night a week. Since he sees only one patient that night, he would have to charge each pa-

tient roughly $4,000 (plus tests, special equipment, drugs and nurses) just to meet his annual salary requirements.

This is a conservative estimate. It doesn't cover the losses for the weeks when his practice is preempted by a presidential speech.

The truth is many of Doc Welby's patients today are probably in hock paying the bills from last year's shows. But that's nothing. I've heard that patients have bills left over from six years ago when Dr. Ben Casey operated on them.

"McHale's Navy." "McHale's Navy" had impact
in its day. It inspired "F Troop."

McCarthy, Kevin. See: "The Bull-Running on
Madison Avenue" and "Car Salesman of the Year."

Medical Education at Home.
There is an enormous need for diagnosis and treatment of common ailments on TV shows. When Dr. Kildare and Ben Casey were practicing on television, the viewer could get reasonably educated about common ailments from their shows. There was a direct relationship in those days between the symptoms patients brought into the office and the subject matter on the medical shows the previous night.

None of the heroes in the new medical series like "The Interns," "Medical Center" and the doctors sequence of "The Bold Ones" seem to be dedicated to this area of medicine. They are into spectacular medicine, like heart transplants and liver failure.

For years Dr. Frank Oski of the University of Pennsylvania School of Medicine has been trying to sell the networks a program called "What's My Disease?" or "Diagnosis, Please." Its purpose is to expose television viewers to the romance and excitement of humdrum medicine. According to Oski, who is a professor of pediatrics, the medical game show works like this:

A panel of three general practitioners would be the stars of the show. They would be typical GPs, worried about their patients and the stock market. The moderator, also a physician, would direct the patient-contestant to recite his symptomatology. The patient might say, "I didn't have a fever, but sometimes I felt hot (or cold)."

The disease of the night, Oski explained, would be one that was "in." "Not like elephantiasis," he said. "Something like infectious mononucleosis or hepatitis would be popular with young viewers. Certain types of side effects from the use of drugs, such as weight control pills, are diseases good for ratings."

The panel of doctors would be allowed to ask pertinent questions and examine the patient for five minutes, or the doctor's usual amount of time allotted per patient, whichever is longer. The end of the first part of the show would be signaled by the patient crying out "What's my disease?"

Each doctor's diagnosis, and what he would have charged for

it, would be broadcast to the home audience, but be kept secret from the other doctors on the panel.

In the second round, the doctors would be free to ask for any lab tests they thought the patient should undergo. "There wouldn't be any jabbing of arms for blood or anything like that," Oski said. All possible tests will have been conducted on the patient-contestant in advance. "The educational value of this part of the show," Oski added, "is that the doctor would have the opportunity to explain the reasoning behind the tests he asked for."

After the test results were studied, the moderator would ask "Diagnosis, please?" Viewers at home would be able to analyze the disparity in each doctor's two analyses.

In the third round, the moderator would announce: "In fact, this is what the patient had." He would then give a brief run-down of the true data in the case and lecture on the specific medical problem.

The entertainment values of "What's My Disease?" could be further enhanced by having a guest layman on the panel, one of those individuals who knows all about medicine from studying *Merck's Manual* and the latest in folk remedies, to compete against the professionals.

"The show will expose the toughness of making diagnosis," Oski explained. "The panelists will usually disagree."

"Is that such a good thing?" I asked.

"It will help people recognize the fallibility of everybody's doctor, except their own."

Minow, Newton. Although the TV industry didn't make much of it, May 9, 1971 was the tenth anniversary of Newton Minow's famous speech about American television. Only two of his words are still remembered, but that's a lot for a Federal Communications Commission (FCC) chairman. As part

of my celebration of that landmark in TV history, I read the complete text of the Minow speech for the first time.

Much of the address (delivered at the Thirty-ninth Annual Convention of the National Association of Broadcasters) was inside trade talk. "Your license lets you use the public airwaves as trustees for 180 million Americans," Minow explained. "The public is your beneficiary. If you want to stay on as trustees, you must deliver a decent return to the public—not only to your stockholders. . . . Gentlemen, your trust accounting with your beneficiaries is overdue. Never have so few owed so much to so many."

This was the standard technical mumbo-jumbo of broadcasting, which even the broadcasters don't understand. The part of the speech that made Newton Minow famous as a critic began:

"When television is good, nothing—not the theater, not the magazines or newspapers—is better. But when television is bad, nothing is worse. I invite you to sit down in front of your television set when your station goes on the air and stay there without a book, magazine, newspaper, profit and loss sheet, or rating book to distract you—and keep your eyes glued to that set until the station signs off. I can assure you that you will observe a vast wasteland."

This wasn't just the former chairman's offhand opinion. It obviously was the conclusion of a careful study he had made about television since taking over the FCC a year earlier. "You will see," he explained, "a procession of game shows, violence, audience participation shows, formula comedies about totally unbelievable families, blood and thunder, mayhem, violence, sadism, murder, western badmen, western good men, private eyes, gangsters, more violence, and cartoons. And, endlessly, commercials—many screaming, cajoling and offending."

Minow's speech, to the best of my knowledge, marked the first time an FCC chairman ever went on record as having watched television—a major breakthrough for an agency sometimes known as the Federal Comatose Commission. Usually the commissioners are far too busy watching the lobbyists to watch

94

the programs. Minow was appalled by what he saw on TV, but he soon got over it. He left his post as critic-in-residence and found a job as counsel for one of the three cultural oases in the wasteland (CBS).

I don't mean to imply there was anything improper in this. Former FCC commissioners often go to work in the industry they had been regulating. This is an honorable tradition dating back to Henry A. Bellows, who in 1932 graduated from the Federal Radio Commission to a vice-presidency at CBS. Actually, only about a half-dozen ex-commissioners have joined the networks, but many others have become station owners or joined law firms that are part of the FCC bar. The industry has long been dangling offers before the present critic-in-residence, Nicholas Johnson.

In the category of pugnacious FCC chairmen, my own favorite is E. William Henry, who succeeded Minow in the early 1960's. His most memorable fight was an attempt to limit the amount of airtime for commercials. Congress immediately passed a bill taking away the commission's right to meddle in this area. "It took thirty-two seconds," one industry veteran recalls. "The fastest piece of legislation in history." Henry concluded that the FCC had made a gallant fight, that the people were now aware of the problem, and that his next target would be loud commercials.

Misleading Political Commercials.

Roger Ailes, who is best known for his work in using TV to sell the American people Richard Nixon in 1968, wasn't very impressed with the smear tactics used in 1970. "The things people are screaming about are on such an elementary level," explained Ailes, who had just finished up a busy fall selling senators and governors to the people, "when you think of what the politicians could have done."

The roughest stuff in 1970 was the law-and-order commercials, the rage in so many states one would think they were bought by politicians from a catalog. Usually they began with a shot of the distinguished opponent, a liberal, smiling. Dissolve to the Chicago Seven. A picture of the smiling candidate again. Dissolve to shots of students throwing rocks. Picture of the smiling candidate again.

The commercials were implying there was a connection between the liberals and the turmoil in society. Because the candidate was smiling, the candidate approved of rock-throwing. In the more leisurely worlds of false argument, such as in the printed word or debates, this is a highly developed art called "guilt by association." In the faster-paced TV commercial world, the image-builders have time to make only the association, and they hope you find the guilt by yourself.

"We have to be very careful when we accuse politicians of being dirty on tepid material like that," Ailes explained. "It's liable to trigger a backlash. Next election they can say, 'No more of this nice-guy stuff.' "

In the next campaign Ailes wouldn't be surprised to see candidates hiring a camera crew to follow their opponents around. Whenever the opponent went to a ball game, for example, the photographer would take shots of him with his fists in the air, cheering on the home team.

"What for?"

"They cut the film," Ailes explained, "take out the fist shot and superimpose it in a crowd of blacks. In a race where racial tension was high, they might juxtapose that shot with some stock footage of Eldridge Cleaver in Algeria. A great endorsement for his opponent."

Ailes said the camera crew would try to film a lot of *cinéma vérité* stuff of the candidate entering basement doorways. "Works wonders for implying cell meetings."

And it's very important to film his opponent shaking hands with workers in front of the factory gates, smiling against the smokestacks. "With a little editing," Ailes explained, "that could make a terrific endorsement for pollution.

"Of course, if they just wanted to embarrass their opponent," Ailes said, "all they would have to do is follow him on the banquet circuit. By shooting long enough, they'd be bound to get pictures of a piece of food falling out of his mouth. Then they'd be able to paint him as a slob. The value of that is that it turns off the upper social classes, the money people. It's just one of those things—those people don't want to contribute money to a guy with a piece of asparagus on his shirt."

At the same time, Ailes explained, they would have an audio team taping the opponent's speeches for use in commercials. "The speech would be cut and interspersed with a woman's voice. If you filter a public speech properly, it sounds like a tapped phone call and illicit as all hell."

Critics of TV political advertisements say they mislead the people. That may be so. But all commericals do that; it may even be their function. Why is there no agitation for legislation limiting the number of soap or aspirin commericals?

If a politician is lying in a commerical, at least he is limited to 60 seconds. In the old days of political speeches to the voters, there was no limit to the perfidy. Debates and press conferences on TV—two other ways to keep the voters informed—also have drawbacks. Despite all the talk about the negative impact of television, people will continue to vote in a discriminating way —on the basis of a man's religion, his sex appeal, and his party.

Monday Night at the Movies. It's hard
to say which network show using old movies is more creative: "NBC Monday Night at the Movies," "The CBS Thursday Night Movies," "The CBS Friday Night Movies," "NBC Saturday Night at the Movies" and "The ABC Sunday Night Movie." What I find most creative about the genre is the titles.

While trying to find out who invented the name "NBC Monday Night at the Movies," I happened to mention my unabashed

97

admiration for the title. "It's terrific isn't it?" an NBC executive said. "We like it because it has great flexibility."

The genius who first thought of the basic title back in 1961 was an NBC programming executive named David Levy. He was fired—not for lack of imagination—shortly before his revolutionary concept in show titles ("Saturday Night at the Movies," as the first of this type was known) went on the air.

Levy didn't invent the idea of putting old movies on TV. That began the first day the medium was invented. His contribution was breaking with the concept of the "Late Show" and "Early Show"—the two tradtional times for movies—and having the guts to put old movies on in prime time. A lot of industry experts thought we wouldn't watch old movies in prime time, no matter how much creativity went into writing the title of the show.

After Levy was vindicated, ABC tried running an old movie in prime time. The network innovation broke new ground by running its show—first called "Hollywood Special"—on Sunday night. In January, 1962, ABC decided to rename the show.

Much of the credit for all the creativity in the field of naming movie shows should go to Mort Werner, the man who replaced David Levy as programming head at NBC. His list of credits includes "Monday Night at the Movies," "Tuesday Night at the Movies" and "Wednesday Night at the Movies."

"Wednesday Night at the Movies," despite the fresh ring to it, isn't a new movie show on NBC next season. It is the name of an old NBC program moved to Tuesday night and renamed "Tuesday Night at the Movies." The original "Tuesday Night at the Movies" was then moved to "Monday Night at the Movies." All of these network machinations don't mean much to viewers, who must love old movies. Werner, I heard the other day, secretly hates movies. He thinks they aren't very creative. He doesn't even like NBC's "World Premiere" movies; the ones especially made for TV. Most critics seem to agree with him. Original movies just aren't old movies.

Perhaps the most creative act in the history of movie show

title-writing took place in 1965 at CBS. They were the first to put their own network name in the title, as in "The CBS Thursday Night Movies." The idea, I suppose, was to distinguish their old movies from the other networks' old movies.

It was something of a surprise when CBS got into the old-movie business in the first place. Only a year earlier, the network had been assuring viewers in newspaper stories that old movies would never be on CBS. The network attacked the concept of old movies for stifling creativity in the medium. "What they obviously meant to say," according to a former NBC executive, "is that NBC's old movies would never be on CBS. They somehow found their own."

After CBS shook up the old-movie establishment by rewriting the title slightly, there were discussions at NBC about whether they should follow suit. The transcripts of these high level talks are still not available to the press. But the arguments must have been persuasive, as all the networks are now following CBS.

The fancy writing in titles, pioneered by CBS, has its amusing aspects for viewers in cities where stations use more than one network's programs. In Birmingham, viewers watching the NBC station on a recent Saturday night saw a show titled "The CBS Thursday Night Movies."

Morton's Lemon Cream Pie. A hit of the
premiere of "The Great American Dream Machine" was actor Marshall Efron's piece in the test kitchen, where he showed how to make a lemon cream pie using all the ingredients listed on a frozen lemon cream pie box. After bumping around a lot of beakers and flasks containing all the wholesome chemical ingredients, Efron, like a master TV chef, held up the finished product: in this case, a box of Morton's lemon cream pie. (An even closer inspection of the box would have turned up the fact that the Morton Pie Company is a subsidiary of ITT Corporation, a major potential contributor to public television.)

99

When this culinary note was first announced through the grapevine, everybody marveled at "The Great American Dream Machine's" courage. The ITT pie people might sue.

It was hard to imagine on what grounds ITT might sue, though. Morton's lemon cream pies definitely didn't contain either lemons or cream, as Efron reported. That's why the pies stay factory-fresh for seven or eight months. That they sell so well must be proof that ITT is only giving the public what it wants.

The dramatic moment on TV arrived. Efron looked appropriately proud as he held up the box.

At first I was a little surprised by the camera work on this final scene. Not only couldn't I read the fine print on the box, where it gave ITT a free plug, but I couldn't read the word "Morton's" either. However, anybody who really wanted to read those things could have held a magnifying glass against the screen and picked out the brand name easily enough. Show the viewer everything, runs the basic principle in this moderate step forward, but don't let him see it.

When the day comes that television is allowed to use more sex in its programs, "The Great American Dream Machine" has provided a clue to how the medium will deal with the new permissiveness. The networks will tell us we're watching the hard-core stuff, but for some reason we won't be able to see it.

Mother (blip)! See "Blip."

Movie Festivals. Once a week a network should run the last ten minutes of the previous week's movies in prime time. Old movies were made for viewing in theaters. They usually start off fast, then bog down in the frills of character development. Once they have you in the theater, there's nothing to do but sit there patiently, waiting for the story to zoom to its dramatic finish. But watching these pre-TV movies in bed, many viewers fall asleep. You'd be amazed at how many people are walking around wondering how such all-time film greats as "The Vampire and the Girl" ended.

A festival of the last ten minutes of all the month's previous movies also would appeal to the people who enjoy reading the last three pages of mysteries.

Movie of the Week. "Movie of the Week" on Tuesday nights on ABC has been one of TV's biggest hit series for a number of reasons. First, it has the word "Movie" in the title. Secondly, it's the only show with the word "Movie" in the title on Tuesday nights. The series has so much going for it the actual movie rarely seems to be the criterion for watching.

"We're not interested in movies with ideas," a network executive once explained about the medium's philosophy. "We just want a film that will hook people when they see the first thirty seconds of excerpts on their screens."

101

"My Three Sons"'s Contribution to Western Civilization.

"My Three Sons" is an important example of what other critics call "escapist junk," but which I consider an important function of TV. The Douglas family—and their neighbors the Nelsons (Ozzie and Harriet), the Andersons ("Father Knows Best") and the Donna Reed Family—was the place where a viewer could escape from the reality of his own house. On that Great Block in the Sky, fathers never yelled at their kids, mothers never threw dishes or uttered profanities, nobody ever hit his children unreasonably or worried about making a living. It was a terrific make-believe world where a father always put his arm around his troubled child's shoulders and said, "What's the matter, son (or daughter) ?" There actually might have been a few families like that in real life, statistically speaking, but I never knew one.

National Obscenity Test.

I have a new scheme for getting mature films on TV. Let us suppose that nobody had seen *I am Curious (Yellow)*. FCC Chairman Burch might take this film to, say, NBC, and suggest, "We would like

you to run this film in place of your usual dog on Tuesday night."
The network might say, "We'd rather not. But if we don't do
it, somebody else will."

A few minutes before the film went on the air, Dean Burch
would go on the air and deliver a promo for the show. "You
are about to participate in a National Obscenity Test. If you or
your family would rather not participate in a test, please turn
your television set off." Playing on the patriotism of the television audience, I would image this might be the most effective
plug for a show in the history of the medium.

To protect its high moral position in the community, the president of the network could then come on the air and announce,
"The views expressed on the following program are not neces-
sarily those of the network." At each break for a commercial,
the network would reiterate the point: "This program is presented as a public service."

Those who were horrified by what they saw, the network
would encourage to join their local private censorship group.

National Unusual Television. The prob-
lem with educational television used to be its name. Image-wise,
"educational television" projected the negative feeling it was
teaching something. The programs always sounded like they
would be heavy. Even the idea of turning the dial to the local
NET outlet induced fatigue.

The educational television establishment was aware of the
weakness in its generic name. In 1969, a movement began to sub-
stitute the word "public" for "educational." While that was a
step in the right direction, thus far it has succeeded only in
giving the fine old word "public" a bad reputation. "Corporation
for Public Broadcasting"—the organization which Congress created to lead us into the golden age of educational TV—was a
total disaster as a name. It sounds more like a trust or a mutual

fund than a fun-thing. Psychologically people fear that with a name like that you are going to try to sell them something.

Public television (née educational television), should probably adopt the name "unusual television." But since the call letters National Unusual Television might be a source of derision, why not just call it "entertainment television"? The commercial networks have no monopoly on the word "entertainment."

The strategy in all of this is to confuse the viewers: NET will seem like just another one of four entertainment networks. This may seem sneaky, but at least one of the three existing networks might not feel too badly about it. ABC would no longer be last in the ratings—at least for awhile.

New Trends in Football Reporting.

There was a strong trend in 1971–72 televised games to give detailed reports of injuries to ballplayers, especially football players. It is estimated that .1 per cent of aired sports commentary this year has been devoted to such reports. This is up 549 percent over last year, despite the recession. Ligaments, cartilages, tendons, kneecaps and Achilles heels are among the parts of the anatomy enjoying national exposure.

"If the percentage of medical reports continues to rise," explained one network official, worried about the trend, "it is projected that by 1981 more than 100 percent of sports commentary will be devoted to injuries, ordinary and exotic."

By next season, some authorities predict, the network games will have a feature called "Injury of the Week." "What will it be?" announcers will ask excitedly, "To whom? And to what part of the body?" The more serious TV football fans may start betting on the injuries, instead of the game.

When the players are introduced before the game, the experts could show their X-rays instead of their pictures. Analysis of their medical reports would replace the old statistics about yardage gained. For the half-time show, they could switch to Mt.

Sinai Hospital where Howard Cosell would give the play-by-play of last week's operation, interview the surgeons and give the instant replay of the incision. Eventually the sport itself might be superceded by medical reports, and the games could be eliminated entirely.

Your sports reporter believes the fans love this trend. It's substantive proof that the game of football is really violent, not just a bunch of grown men falling on the grass. The medical reports serve the same function as casualty lists in a war. TV viewers would have been bored with the Vietnam war long ago without the weekly statistics on the news shows.

News and Commercials. The impact that results from juxtaposing the bad news of the news with the good news of the commercials has never been studied thoroughly. Something must happen, I am convinced, when a television viewer hears about a woman being raped in the East Village, a fire in the South Bronx, and then the newscaster says, "We'll be back with the earthquake in Peru after this brief word from our sponsor."

It isn't easy to keep our minds on a My Lai massacre when a moment later we see the good news that we can drive a 1971 car on a secluded beach with that beautiful model in the front seat. If commercials ran five or ten seconds longer, we might see that wonderful machine stuck in the sand and the beautiful girl walking forlornly off into the sunset in search of a phone booth to call the AAA for a tow truck. But that's not anything a biased commercial would go into.

The commericals also contribute to a moral obliqueness that may be one of our strengths as a people. The other night, for example, viewers in the New York area saw a news report about three kids being burned to death in a ghetto fire. The next commercial happened to be a message about Crest toothpaste. The kid who rushed up to his father had—thank God!—no cavities, but his father was a fireman. Was this a sick joke, an innocent

senator might have asked? Of course, it was just one of those
ironies of the juxtaposition of bad news and good news that go
unreported every day. The only standing order, explained an
executive at the local station that ran the fire story and Crest
commercial side-by-side, is to kill airline commercials on days
when an airplane crashes.

Three thousand people died in Peru? So what's on "The Late
Show"? The networks are against the Laos incursion? So what?
The network news show is the best defense the human mind has
yet invented to keep the masses from getting angry about anything. How bad can anything be if it will go away in a minute?
A newspaper story about terrible news is fixed solidly on the
page; it is still there to be read after a distraction. With TV, you
turn your head and miss an earthquake.

News Interviewing, or Talking to One's Self.
In the early days of TV journalism, it was
fairly common to tune in a news show for enlightenment and
discover a correspondent like NBC's Hugh Downs interviewing
NBC correspondent Martin Agronsky on, say, the meaning of

the national elections. "It was always an exclusive interview," explained Calvin Trillin, the writer and TV viewer. "No other network shared Mr. Agronsky and his remarks appeared in no newspaper. I saw Mr. Downs interviewing Mr. Agronsky several times the same week. I also watched Mr. Downs interviewing John Chancellor, who himself used to interview Mr. Agronsky, when he couldn't get Sander Vanocur, who was often busy preparing for the questions he thought Chet Huntley might throw at him."

This brilliantly simple device of having your correspondents grant interviews to each other was one of television's major contributions to journalism. "For all its talk about printing all the news," Trillin observed, *"The New York Times* has never thought of sending James Reston out to interview Harrison Salisbury."

Before long, of course, the idea of one correspondent interviewing another was improved upon by having six correspondents on at the same time. In fact, this has become a ritual all three networks indulge in at the turn of the year.

The implication behind all the visiting around on the news shows is that the correspondents had been coy with the public during their regular stints on camera earlier in the year. They still had some privileged information they were holding back from us. All that was needed was the right incisive interviewer to loosen up their tongues before thirty million viewers.

This hasn't been the case. The amount of hard and soft news (or gossip) that Cronkite and Collingswood managed to worm out of their teammates during the hour-long grillings could be written on the head of a transistor. Networks go to great expense to bring the correspondents home, but what it adds up to is a lot of moving furniture around pretending that it is a change of view. And it's a shame. When the correspondents sit around a bottle of scotch at a bar, they inevitably have a fund of interesting stories to tell about all the things they weren't able to say on the air. But, for some reason, the juicy stuff slips their minds at the year-end wrap-ups.

Ultimately the correspondents on these seminars give the impression of men who are pretty much talking to themselves, what has been called in physics "the barber shop effect." One looks into the mirror on the wall in a barber shop and sees the reflection of a barber cutting hair in the rear mirror; the mirror images are projected infinitely. It's exciting stuff visually, but you don't learn much about what is really going on.

Newspaper Listings. In place of program list-
ings, which tell only a small part of what is on TV anyway, friends of the medium are urging that newspapers begin listing what commercial broadcasting is all about: the commercials. They cost more per minute to produce than the programs. They are more controversial than the programs. They evoke a greater range of emotions (from disgust to an urge to run right out and buy something). The funny commericals have more laughs than some situation comedies. And the dramas are more serious and more relevant to the viewer's life.

At first, advocates of the new, improved newspaper listings say, they should be only slightly rewritten, like this:

THE TONITE SHOW (NBC, 11:30 PM). Appearing with Johnny tonight are Chevvy Camaro, Calgon Bleach, Prince

Spaghetti, the hilarious Mobil Rocker Assembly and controversial black Preparation X.

But eventually the listings would drop all mention of the programs:

ABC. 7:18 PM. In this taut chiller an emotionally disturbed young homemaker is taunted and threatened by a drawerful of shirts whose collars are mysteriously stained. Repeat.

CBS. 8:22 PM. Ralph Bellamy and Joan Bennett star in "Tired Blood." In color.

ABC. 9:02 PM. The fate of a marriage rests with a Good Samaritan and her bottle of Ultramouth gargle when an impetuous beau tells his fiancee that her breath reeks. Repeat.

NBC. 9:56 PM. Phlegm threatens to invade an entire sinus passage, resisting conventional sprays until an obscure scientist tries his miraculous nasagraph. Premiere.

Noble Causes. A friend was so impressed by TV's massive coverage planned for Earth Day 1970, he announced that to help fight environmental decay he would give up smoking. Since he wasn't sure that he'd be able to do it, he also said that he was planning to hold his breath for one minute. "Let somebody else have my air," explained Richard R. Lingeman, the amateur ecologist. Others did their bit by giving up television for the day.

Novak, Kim. When I asked an ABC public relations man what Kim Novak would be doing in "This Land is Mine"—the network's documentary study of all that is still beautiful in America—he told me she opens the show standing on the rocks off the coast of California and shouting at the waves, "Marvin

109

Kitman, Marvin Kitman." I decided to watch the April 6 program anyway.

Actually the publicized shouting match with the surf at Big Sur turned out to be, on closer inspection, Miss Novak singing. Given the roar of the waves and her wispy voice, it was hard to make out all the words. But it seemed to be a protest song against the fickleness of the tide. It always goes in and out, she observed. "Watching our love come out/watching our love go in," went one moving refrain. Whatever good Miss Novak did for the fight against water pollution at Santa Barbara, she failed to solve the noise pollution problem at Big Sur.

"Kim Novak is an actress," the ABC News narrator explained for the benefit of a generation of hearts unbroken by her *Jeanne Eagels*. "She is in love with the sea and the land. This is the story of a love affair."

Well, that answered the faithful's questions about whom she has been dating lately. As the documentary moved restlessly across the mountains, deserts, coasts, and plains—in search of the vast amount of natural beauty remaining—I couldn't help marveling at Kim Novak's condition. Although a bit heavier than the last time I saw her on film, she has withstood the ravages of man better than the rest of our natural resources.

But "This Land Is Mine" added little to the television audience's body of knowledge about the Grand Canyon, Martha's Vineyard, the Georgia marshlands and Jackson Hole. In fact, some viewers may have concluded that the producers were having a love affair with old picture-postcards. I preferred to think of the documentary as a special on Kim Novak, activist.

Fortunately, the cameras, like the tide, kept coming back to Miss Novak's rocks. "When I found this place," she said in a whisper, flinging her hands out toward her home nestled in the foothills of Big Sur, "I knew it was really for me. When I was a kid in Chicago, I used to write poetry. You need inspiration in life. The sea is for me. It's just wild and free. Not endangered."

In the old days when Miss Novak spoke breathlessly and incoherently, I used to think that was just her thing as an actress.

110

Now that programs like hers have made me aware of the dangers of the environment, I found myself troubled by her shortness of breath. Does she have emphysema?

"Things that are important to me," she explained, derailing my train of thought, "are animals. Maybe it's because I never married. My horse. My donkeys. I like to ride. The deer—come free. The only thing I can't eliminate are the jets."

I didn't understand what she was talking about, but I didn't want her to stop. And she never did, in the all-too-brief moments the cameras were on her, saying things like, "The place for me is out in the wild with my animals."

"Who does she dress like that for?" asked a more objective authority on Kim Novak, my wife. "Her cats or her dogs?" For a woman who only lives with animals, she did seem to dress like a movie star.

Yet at moments, as she talked profoundly about her love for the land and sea, she seemed truly wedded to nature. "There is so much beauty in the world," she gasped. "No man can ever recreate a tree. The redwoods. They must have seen and heard so much. They just stand there. If man could learn the tolerance of the tree." Maybe Kim Novak is preparing to run for governor of California in the upcoming election.

Nudism. See "History of the Nude in Television."

Old Folks. Harvey Jacobs and Gary Belkin told me the other day about an exciting new show they are getting ready to pitch at the networks, called "Senility Street."

"We began thinking of a show for the group that doesn't have much on TV," Belkin explained.

"Senility Street" will be informational and instructional. "But fun," Jacobs added. "We do this through humor and preaching open hostility toward youth. Instead of Oscar, for example, a sullen teenager lives in the Senility Street garbage can. Occasionally a teenage idol will be hung in effigy from a Senility Street light pole. The humor will be very subtle."

"One of the most popular parts of the show," Belkin predicted, "will be a daily phone call from a kid who finally called his mother."

Outrage. See "Selling of the Pentagon."

Out-Takes. Instead of turning over out-takes (unused footage from re-shootings of a scene) to Congress, CBS ought to play them on the air some night for everybody to see. Not only would this be a relatively cheap documentary for CBS, but it would take away some of the mystique about out-takes. Once the Congress and the public sat through twelve takes of a TV correspondent trying to get just the right note of warmth into a report ("Lawrence, Kansas, is a quiet town today, except for those who are burying their dead"), you could never interest them in unused material again.

The Pentagon Videotapes. After the Supreme Court's decision on the Pentagon papers, reaffirming the media's rights to print secrets under the First Amendment, government-secret fans expected that TV news would rush to put a lot of exciting secrets on the air. This has not been the case. "All we've seen on TV news this summer," one disappointed government-secrets fan said, "is Walter Cronkite. He's no secret."

A top television news official explained why. "The Supreme Court decision came at a bad time for television—just before the summer. Since we hadn't run any secrets in the first place, we couldn't rerun them during the summer."

Television news, a reliably informed source assured me, wants to run government secrets like the other media. But the networks have exceptionally high standards.

There are two kinds of government secrets, as far as television is concerned: prime-time secrets and fringe-time secrets. None of the government secrets making the rounds of network news departments these days are good enough to fit into either category.

"What's a prime-time secret?" I asked.

"The FBI giving lie detector tests to State Department officials," the network official explained. "But since Kissinger has been running the State Department the people over there don't know anything anyway."

Bearers of government secrets, I was told, don't understand the special requirements of the medium. "For TV to run secrets," the source explained, "they have to come in multiples of thirteen to fit into the programming cycle. One fellow last week came around with eleven secrets. If he comes back with two more, we'll consider running them."

The worst kind of secrets, as far as television is concerned, are those Xerox copies of the Pentagon papers, which the newspapers ran. "All we could do to cover that story was run the front pages of newspapers indicted for revealing the secrets," the network executive complained. "Stills of columns of gray print aren't exciting.

"As long as government and their officials continue to keep records in writing, they can't expect to get their secrets on the network news shows as easily as in the papers. If Ellsberg, or whoever leaked those things to the public, had his wits about him, he would have operated with a portable Sony video-recorder. We'd have been happy to take those secrets."

I don't want to give the impression that television doesn't feel any sense of responsibility about keeping the public informed. After government secrets like the Pentagon papers are printed in the newspapers, they are published in a Bantam book. The author is then always invited to appear on "The Today Show." That's how secrets get on TV.

Pilots. In the course of petitioning the Federal Communications Commission for relief from one of its new rules—the reduction of network "prime time" programming from four to three hours to encourage more local shows—Screen Gems revealed the cost of making a pilot, that *sine qua non* of selling a series to the networks. According to Screen Gems' accountants, a half-hour pilot now costs "in excess of $360,000," and the average half-hour program in a series—*after* the pilot has been sold—cost $105,000. They must have believed the FCC did not know these elementary facts. They were probably right.

While Screen Gems has managed to sell nineteen film series to the networks since 1965, its petition declared that it has produced forty-six pilots during this period. "Thus, the true pilot cost to be absorbed by each series [sold] is roughly two-and-a-half times the cost of its own pilot, or close to $900,000 per half-hour series in today's market." This figure does not take into account the cost of the very substantial number of projects that fail to reach the pilot stage. (Alan King once said about the risk factor, "I've lost more pilots than the Luftwaffe.") It also does not include what Screen Gems described as "the expense of maintaining a staff of high salaried personnel to create . . . properties."

$900,000 is as good an argument as any for viewers to suspend judgment on new shows, whose pilots are often shown as first episodes during the premiere weeks of a new season. We won't know how good—or bad—the series really is until the networks begin showing us some of those $100,000 episodes.

The fallacy of deciding anything after watching the premiere is further demonstrated by the saga of "Compound 45," a situation comedy about American fliers incarcerated in an Italian prisoner-of-war camp. One of the best pilots in recent history, it was screened for executives at NBC the year "Hogan's Heroes" was bought by CBS. Even executives who only saw part of it were rolling in the aisle. Yet NBC didn't buy it because it raised a serious question: If the pilot was this good, they asked, how would they be able to sustain it the second week?

A producer who makes a hilarious pilot is cutting his own

throat. This explains why premieres shy away from excellence in favor of mediocrity.

Pooled News.

A Ford Foundation official, who studies things like this in his free time, once conducted a survey which found that there actually was a .007 percent difference in the three networks' coverage of news. "A major story one day was the return of a group of American students who defied the State Department by going to Cuba to cut cane," the foundation man recalled. "The three networks went to the airport and they all came back with the same camera shots of the student.

"I used to think the three network news editors called a conference in the morning and planned the day's coverage," he said. "But that's not true. They don't have to. They all think alike."

This conversation was in the back of my mind the week I had lunch with Al Levin, the documentary-maker. Levin believes that the networks could save the most money by completely eliminating such costly broadcasting frills as the entire network news departments. He proposes the establishment of a single, pooled, super-network news department.

"When the administration calls a press conference," Levin explained of the advantages of the TV news trust or commune, "all three networks today have to cover it. That is two too many reporters. Under the new system, the extra men would be free for other assignments. They might even find out what led to the calling of the press conference in the first place. The real story is often behind the scenes."

Presidential Press Conferences.

The function of the TV presidential press conference is for Washington reporters to show their bosses that they're working. A more effective use of the visual medium would be for the reporters to wear T-shirts with their names and papers emblazoned on the back. Some papers might even want to run a line or two of copy on the shirts, such as "We endorsed Nixon editorially in 1968."

Then, like basketball and football players at the start of TV games, the reporters could run into the East Room one at a time before the press conference began, be introduced, take a bow and their seats. When the president finally made his entrance, the reporters will have had time to organize their thoughts. At the last press conference, two reporters even asked the same hard question.

Maybe what has been keeping them from organizing their thoughts is that they're really working for a rival medium. "Jumping up all the time," explained Peter Lisagore of the Chicago *Daily News* during a panel discussion on the Public Broadcasting Service's "Washington Week in Review," "we are in danger of bumping our heads on the cameras. If we ask good questions, we should be paid Actor's Equity scales."

The whole institution of the TV press conference has come under attack lately. But there's nothing wrong with the institution, as far as the president is concerned. Historically, when a president goes before the people, he always wants to say as little as possible.

There's probably nothing wrong with the institution, as far as the public is concerned, which couldn't be remedied by a hard-hitting interview with a real TV reporter *after* the press conference.

My nominee for such an important assignment would be Howard Cosell, the ABC sportscaster. Anybody who saw Cosell questioning Muhammed Ali in the ring after the telecast of the Ali–Bonaventura fight can imagine how such an interview might run.

The president, still sweating from his TV wrestling match with the Washington press corps, would be stopped by Cosell before he left the stage. "This was the big one tonight, Mr. President. All eyes were on you. And wouldn't you have to admit that you were terrible out there, sir?"

"Well, I want to make this clear, Howard, it's a free country, and every newsman is entitled to his opinion."

"Let's not be coy about this, Richard," Cosell might press on. "You showed the nation some fancy footwork on the first three questions. But I'm sure you'd like to use this opportunity to tell the people that you were a disgrace to your profession."

"Let me be candid about this, Howard. Nobody is perfect."

"All right, Dick," Cosell might continue, putting his arm around the president's shoulders. "At the beginning of the year they all laughed when you said you would come in under the budget. How do you explain not having fulfilled that commitment?"

"We still have a few days left, Howard. Ask me about this later in the year."

"Is it true, Dandy Dick, that you are planning to dump Spiro Agnew in 1972? I was having lunch with my old friend, Hubert Humphrey, and he told me off the record that you're thinking of making Robert Taft Jr. your running mate. Nobody likes to see a great American like Spiro go into an unmarked political grave. But he does have a law degree, has made important contacts in Washington, and I just have the feeling that once retired to private life, he'll become a millionaire."

"Howard, I'm exhausted. Couldn't I just say hello to all the folks in Key Biscayne and San Clemente and be allowed to go home to my wife?"

"One last question, Dashing Dick. When will you be holding your next press conference?"

"You'll be the last to know, Howard."

"Thank you, Mr. President, for putting us on."

Principles of Programming. "The Whale Hunters of Fayal" on NBC was a great documentary, especially

if you were interested in whales. Unfortunately, I only saw part of the documentary, which starred the voice of José Ferrer and some unidentified whales off the island of Fayal, one of the Azores. The same night, at the same time 7:30–8:30 P.M. on a Thursday night, ABC was showing Jacques Cousteau's "Return of the Sea Lions." If there's anything I am interested in more than whales, it's sea lions.

As I tried to catch both the whales and the sea lions—they both got away—I found myself thinking about how it happened that two of the greatest programs in the annals of the sea on TV were on the air opposite each other. Is it possible there is tradition that at 7:30 P.M. on Thursdays viewers secretly want to go down to the sea on TV—one of those industry myths that everybody knows about except me? Television viewers do have some group habits which have been charted by social scientists—such as leaving the room during commercials.

One theory is that the masterpiece on whaling and Cousteau's rerun of a masterpiece on sea lions happened to go on the air at the same time by what we call in the business "a coincidence." There are just so many openings in a schedule in any given week—maybe twenty or so—and by pure chance they wound up competing for the same nautical crowd. In case there was less interest in the subject than anticipated, this line of reasoning goes, the two networks would go down together, like drowning men hanging on to each other.

There are enough cases of other such coincidences to give this theory some weight. I've noticed that all the networks seem to

have independently decided to put news shows on the air at 11 P.M. The same thing is true at 7 P.M. Late night talk shows always seem to go on the air at 11:30 P.M. My guess, however, is that it is not as coincidental as it all seems. What always amazes me about the medium is that there are still so many hours when different types of shows are allowed to compete with each other during a week.

Print on TV. Usually there is not enough on the screen at any one time to occupy the human mind. Especially for young people who have grown up with TV, or the viewers who watch television due to no fault of their own, such as unemployment.

The printed word is under-utilized in TV technology. I can see no reason why news shows couldn't run news stories in print continuously on the bottom of the screen. The anchorman would give the headlines and the lead paragraphs; the crawl, moving like the stock market transactions on the screen in your broker's office, would carry the stories in greater depth. I think this will prove such a mind-bending experience that eventually there will be a demand for a ribbon of print on all the entertainment shows, too.

Can you sports fans imagine what a public service it would be to get the latest night game baseball scores during "Mannix"? With print, even daytime television can become a meaningful experience. Classified ads could be run at the bottom of the screen with organ accompaniment.

The greatest potential for print may be in the talk show. Say an author appears on a TV talk show, which sometimes happens. The bottom of the screen could be used to give viewers excerpts from the guest's book. A whole novel could be digested without losing the thread of "The Merv Griffin Show."

120

Public Television Poster Girls. The possibility of having public television raise money by classifying itself as a disease is being explored. "The Public TV Poster Girl" could be a little girl with thick glasses from watching too much bad television. Public TV wouldn't settle for just the proceeds of the TV charity drives, but would insist on administering the fund raising itself. That's where the big money is.

Purge. A change of personnel in television is often like one of those changes that take place in Russian history.

Beginning December 7, 1970, Frank Reynolds' name was never mentioned again in the title of ABC's "The Evening News with Frank Reynolds and Howard K. Smith." His picture was gone from the screen. Gone as well were those advertisements which explained what a swell team Reynolds and Smith made, back in the days when they went together like Huntley and Brinkley. His signature disappeared from the one-minute commentaries. And nobody knows what crime Reynolds committed.

It was left to Frank Reynolds himself to tell fans of ABC's seven o'clock news that the most important dumping of an anchorman since CBS threw Walter Cronkite overboard in 1969 was in the works. "Due to circumstances beyond my control," he said in his commentary, "the unemployment statistics rose yesterday."

Nevertheless, Reynolds appeared dismayed by the news in the papers of the day before that Harry Reasoner of CBS had been hired by ABC, as any reporter would be after missing a major story—like his own replacement.

The Real Thing.
The last time I saw Raquel Welch on television was on ABC's Academy Award show, where she was presenting the prize for "the best special effects," a sight gag that drew one of the biggest laughs of the night.

Raquel Welch is the prettiest thing to happen to television since Tony Curtis. One of her major talents is the ability to stand up on stage without pitching over. I never grow tired of watching her do that.

Still, I was curious about what Coca-Cola saw in Raquel Welch to make the staid, conservative Southern company want to sponsor "Raquel," her first television special. Was it the way she stood up, her singing, her dancing, her gift of gab?

"Raquel" features the so-called Charles Schultz Ending. It has no ending. The show does not have a beginning or middle either. What it does have is the actress singing and dancing her way across the world. One song starts on the steps of the Temple of the Moon on the Street of the Dead in Yucatan and winds up—three countries and five costume changes later—in Europe. "It's a free-form floating experience," Coke's agency man explained. "CBS doesn't understand it. They've never had a musical variety show where the hostess doesn't say something like, 'My next guest is...'"

Everything about the $400,000 special, which took 105 days to shoot, is understandable if you keep in mind that its primary

122

purpose is to introduce Coke's new look. What fascinates me is the thinking behind the corporate decision to make Raquel Welch the pitchwoman for this product.

Coca-Cola is a very secretive company. For a hundred years or so they have managed to hide the secret formula to what's in the bottle; for all we know it's still the same old nineteenth century taste. What is known is that apparently sometime in 1970 the Coke people decided they had to do something really innovative, like redesigning their cartons. Research must have shown that a lot of illiterates drink Coke. If they saw Coke in a new package, they might not know it was the same old Coke.

To advertise the new package, there had to be a new image. The soft drink company decided to go with a bright, new, flashing personality who, in the public's mind, had nothing to do with old-fashioned virtues, such as purity, or Coke.

The image Raquel Welch projects—and I blush to say this, it's so obvious—is a million miles from Coke's old image of the college coeds sipping soda in a local sweet shoppe. She represents drinking Coke in a divorce court. No matter how Raquel does her hair she always looks like the other woman. I suppose some women will identify with her in this special. They will say: "Gee she is just like me. Maybe I would like Coke?"

What is so confusing about Raquel Welch as Coke's new image is that she doesn't seem to be the Real Thing. She represents sexual abandonment in the public's mind. But privately she is said to lead an impeccable home life. When she travels to Vietnam, she spends her spare time dropping in on orphanages. When she says she didn't know her next movie, *Myra Breckinridge,* was filled with filth and unspeakable orgies, I believe her. She probably hasn't read the book. When she denies she used the four-letter words in that *Playboy* interview, I'm sure they misquoted her. The campaign to give Coke the image of a wild soft drink, then, is a kind of put-on.

Reasoner, Harry. Harry Reasoner made a major contribution to TV journalism as the host of "The CBS Sunday Night News": he was the first to present the football scores without reading them for the viewer.

This may not seem like much of an accomplishment anywhere but in TV news, an art form still surprisingly reminiscent of radio with pictures, but letting the eyes go it alone on an important subject like football scores took considerable guts. Not even Walter Cronkite or Eric Sevaried, the two giants of TV journalism who were the anchormen on the eleven o'clock Sunday night news prior to Reasoner's taking the job, could figure out how to avoid reading the scores in a visual medium.

A case can be made for the ancient practice. Poor reception in some areas can play havoc with numbers. For example what seems like:

Minnesota Vikings	222
Los Angeles Rams	33

may actually be a ghostly version of:

Minnesota Vikings	22
Los Angeles Rams	3

Another technical problem is that some viewers may experience difficulty in keeping up with the scores as they move on the crawl if they have to read them without the anchorman's help. Since the advent of "Sesame Street," people read numbers a lot faster than they used to, and this is less of a problem than it once was. The numbers are recognized faster; it's not as if football fans had to read a whole sentence.

In 1964, Reasoner and his staff at CBS News held a conference which was to affect the course of football score-reading. Reasoner said he always felt uncomfortable doing them in the traditional way. "Unnecessary, a redundancy," a man who was at the meeting recalls Reasoner arguing. "We could save a little time by not reading them, just showing them."

124

The football scores on the average Sunday night fifteen-minute news show use up forty-five seconds, although on an especially fraught weekend that can go to a full minute. Reasoner argued that the reading-of-the-scores time could better be used to give a line or two of copy about the games.

A compromise was sought. One experiment along these lines had been tried earlier in TV history. "Here are some late scores," George Carlin once reported, "7-2, 3-1, 3-0, 2-1, 9-8." But that time-saver wasn't completely satisfactory.

Reasoner decided to leave out the number part of the score. The teams and the score were flashed on the rear projection screen, as before, but the anchorman limited himself to commenting on who won, such as "The Giants beat the Eagles today."

With the time saved, Reasoner was able to do at least one mini-essay on a game in the charming, wry way that has become known as the Reasoner Style. He's one of the few newsmen who can tell you bad news, like you lost $20 betting on a game, and not make you feel depressed and gloomy.

A typical Reasoner-type observation, after a game in which angry Detroit Lions pelted their coach Harry Gilmer with snow-balls, because the Lions had lost to the New York Giants:

"Scouts for the Detroit Lions and New York Giants have asked for a closer look at the films, having noted that some of the fellows throwing snowballs hit what they were throwing at."

Robbins, Harold. See "Acquisitions."

Rockefeller, John D. III. See "Average Man."

Russell, Jane.

Jane Russell introduced a new approach to answering questions the other night on "The Dick Cavett Show."

A little background on Miss Russell first. She is what the talk show coordinators call "a new face." As far as anybody around the Cavett show could remember, she'd never been on a talk show. Everybody would be thrilled to hear what she had to say, except for the kids who were too young to know who Jane Russell was or what she stood for in the history of American culture.

Yes, her loyal fans said to themselves as she walked out on stage, she is the same Jane Russell. It was those eyes, those unforgettable eyes that haunted a generation.

Cavett began by asking her about *The Outlaw,* the movie that skyrocketed her—as they used to say in the studio press releases —to fame. It took four years (1943–47) to get the movie past the censors, Cavett explained. Miss Russell didn't say anything in defense of the First Amendment or against the fascist Hollywood censors. She just smiled.

"That was some picture," Cavett went on.

She thought about this for some time, and then said, "Yup."

"Was it made by Howard Hawks?"

"Nope."

"That's right . . . it was Howard Hughes?"

Miss Russell was looking down in some embarrassment at the tack the interview was taking, so I didn't hear very clearly what she said next. But it sounded like "Howard who?"

"He was the one who designed a special brassiere for you to wear in the movie?"

"Publicity!" Miss Russell said. Good for her, I thought, she was finally telling it the way it was.

"But he did design an airplane made out of wood during the war," Cavett went on consulting his notes frantically. "It never got off the ground. The plane, I mean, not the brassiere."

"Maybe," she said.

"What was all the furor about *The Outlaw* then?"

"A low-cut blouse."

"People were so easily amused in those days," Cavett said.

That Cavett talks too much, read the notes on my pad. But it was understandable. He looked like he thought he was having trouble sustaining the interview. At one point the long silence gave him such an anxiety attack, he was called upon to blurt out one of his innermost secrets. "I sneaked in to see *The Outlaw*. During the second reel, my voice changed."

Afterwards the Cavett people were a little puzzled by the interview. "She wasn't known as a conversationalist," one man explained. "But we assumed she'd have a lot to talk about. Why else would she go on a talk show?"

Jane Russell is an important discovery because of what she doesn't say—nothing about the Vietnam war, politics, pollution, race, sex, religion.

There have been guests who have been hard to understand, like Fellini. And guests who are impossible to understand, like Dali. Without Jane Russell's saying a word, everybody understands everything. I predict she will start a new vogue in nonverbal communication.

Salaries in Public TV. Congress was stunned
by the news that public television is paying large salaries to its

talent: executives like John W. Macy, Jr., president of the Corporation for Public Broadcasting ($65,000 a year) and performers like Sander Vanocur ($85,000). That's nothing. Wait until the press gets around to revealing public broadcasting's expense accounts.

The positive thing that can be said for large salaries is that they smack of success. By paying large salaries, public television gives the impression that it's a going concern. The American people traditionally admire success.

The San Diego Plan.* The so-called San Diego

Plan was named in honor of the technician at a cable TV station in San Diego who played an unscheduled stag film on the air. A viewer who had fallen asleep during, say, "The Johnny Carson Show," and suddenly awoke to see the mature film on his screen may have thought he had died in his sleep and was in heaven— or hell, depending on his attitude toward sex.

This is an excellent way for stations to test the viewership for odd films. But these sneak previews will upset two major segments of the market: those who will be angry that they had to sit through that kind of thing, and those who will be angry that they missed it.

Saturday Night at the Movies. See

"Monday Night at the Movies."

Schedule Spying. If you wanted to know next

year's TV schedule—one of the worst kept industrial secrets in

* Also known as the Palm Springs, California Plan.

128

the history of the free enterprise system—all you would have to do is hang out around the pool at the Bel Air Hotel in Los Angeles. The basic principle of creative programming is see who producer Aaron Spelling is talking to. When an ABC programming official talks to Spelling, it means that ABC is thinking of a new version of *Mod Squad*. If you've seen one Spelling-Thomas show, you've seem them all.

Spies know that if producer David Victor is seen talking to a network, it means that another *Marcus Welby, M.D.* is in the works. Instead of a doctor show, it may be one about lawyers or a detective. That's the secret. You can tell by the expression on the producer's face whether they have a deal or not.

Anybody could also break the network's top secrets by hanging around the lobby of executive headquarters in New York, such as the CBS or ABC buildings. Look for movie stars who are reportedly having trouble financing their next pictures. At ABC, if the star presses the elevator button for the 37th floor (programming), it means he is still discussing a series. The 39th floor (President Leonard Goldenson's office), the deal is being negotiated. The 40th floor (executive dining room) they're celebrating the signing of the contract. You'd be amazed at how much you can learn just by riding the elevators.

Of course, you would have to be very sharp and know something about the business to become a successful TV espionage agent. If I were running a TV spy ring I would hire only TV executives, some of whom are already on their third network. They are naturally nice to the hundreds of telephone operators, secretaries and clerks who know all the industry's secrets and are dying to tell them to somebody.

Another way to find out the industry's secrets is to escort the would-be TV starlets. They are like bees, picking up bits of secret information from executives and cross-pollinating the whole industry. But who would want to know about TV badly enough to go out with a startlet?

Script Endings.

The standard format for a made-for-TV movie or drama is a beginning, middle, and a happy ending. Sad endings are comparatively rare on commercial TV. There are a lot of sad programs, but that's different.

Every five years or so, there's a movie or drama with a very sad ending. It is this combination of happy and sad endings on the air during the five-year period which gives TV the claim to diversity, often said to be the goal of commercial broadcasting.

The Paul Klein Theory of Broadcasting—named after the former vice-president of audience research and measurement at NBC who went into the computer TV business (his version of a happy ending)—is: "If a show ends sad, people won't come back for it next week." Say there is a case of syphilis on "Marcus Welby," for instance. We know that by the end of the show it will be cured. If somebody has it in a new documentary, we're not sure if it will be cured. A lot of viewers may even think you can catch a problem by watching it, judging by the low ratings for documentaries.

Sea Lions.

See "Principles of Programming."

"The Selling of the Pentagon."

"The Selling of the Pentagon"—a CBS documentary which finally got around to examining the way the Pentagon public relations machinery has been selling us the Vietnam war and the weapons to fight it with—outraged American public opinion. The outrage lasted about three hours. Our capacity for outrage has fallen sharply these days. I can still remember nostalgically the old days when My Lai outraged us for three weeks.

130

About the only person I've heard of who is still outraged about CBS' revelations that the Pentagon manipulates the media and the public with taxpayers' money is Representative F. Edward Hebert of Louisiana. He called writer-producer Peter Davis' documentary "one of the most horrible examples of anti-military presentation" he had ever heard of. Herbert, chairman of the House Armed Services Committee, admitted at the same time that he hadn't even seen the show. I can't take outrage, based on hearsay, seriously.

Severeid, Eric.

The last new development in television news analysis was the debut of Eric Sevareid on CBS. The grand old man of analysis still dominates the field physically. He is the only news analyst whose shoulders don't fit on the TV screen no matter how far the cameras pull back.

The same thing can be said about Clark Kent.

Sevareid tends to repeat himself on the news shows. That's nothing to be ashamed of. History does that all the time. But years of giving both sides of every issue can have an unbalancing effect. On some issues there are actually four sides; on still others there is but one.

Over the years the dean of news analysis has catered to television's need for giving the semblance of change, without there being any, by retreating into incomprehensibility. He has not only influenced the next generation of TV news analysts but also government officials.

The Sinking Fund Foundation Commission.

In 1961 there were 61 public television stations. In 1966 there were 124. Today there are over

200 non-commercial stations bringing culture to the American people. At this rate—doubling every five years—by the year 2071, the United States will have 128,000,000 public television stations. That will be one public television station for every three persons.

This is one conclusion of a report on the future of public television, titled "Television—On or Off?," prepared by the Sinking Fund Foundation Commission. "Almost everyone will be working in public television," explained Tony Geiss, the director of the Foundation. "The rest will be watching it. Hence the commission's concern."

Since excerpts of the commission's preliminary report first appeared on the Public Broadcast Laboratory five years ago, it has been hotly debated in the public TV establishment. Geiss himself has begun to question some of its findings. "Our hypothesis was that the more public TV stations the fewer the listeners. It may be that by the time we reach 2071, nobody will be watching public TV. This is in contrast to the situation that prevails today. Of course we don't have figures to prove any of this yet."

The Sinking Fund Foundation Commission, I should point out, hasn't accomplished too much. Geiss became so discouraged, in fact, he sold out his interest in the Sinking Fund and went to work for the David Frost Show.

The report, however, is still relevant. For example, the report asks, "How do you finance public television?"

"With difficulty," it concludes. To support these findings, the report includes a pie chart showing the source of income for a typical fine eastern PTV station: contributions from federal government, foundations, loan sharks, tin foil drive, skipping lunches, misc. (the deficit is listed in the last category).

"Where can they get more money," the report asks? The Ford Foundation suggests the revenue from a domestic communications satellite. The Carnegie Commission suggests an excise tax on TV sets. CPB suggests Congressional hand-outs. All these methods provide funds, concedes the Sinking Fund

Foundation. But none will improve the *quality* of public TV. Geiss's group proposed a canned laughter tax.

"This would be a per-laugh tax at source on 'family situation comedies' that used canned laughter. The tariff would be especially high when the laughter is for lines like 'Hello,' and 'Yes' or for a small mop-headed dog doing a doubletake. The higher the rating, the bigger the tax. With this levy, the public can't lose. If canned laughter is cut out, commercial TV improves. If it rises, public television gets better."

An alternative is the Dead Body Tax, which Geiss describes as simply a death levy on imaginary slayings: every time an outlaw dies on commerical TV, he finances a poet on public TV. The recent cutback on violence would be compensated for by a Black Side-Kick Tax.

In all fairness, the Sinking Fund points out, public TV should also be taxed for certain practices. Among its recommendations: a Consecutive Interviews Tax (for over 12 in a row). There might also be a Colon Tax (too many shows with split titles like "Luxembourg: Europe's Sleeping Midget," "Shirley Temple: The Middle Years," "High Wind From Secaucus: New Jersey in Revolt") and the Irrelevant Documentary Tax (suddenly at 8:30, a half hour on "The Mountain Mosses of Popocatepetl").

Sloan Commission Report on Cable TV.

In December, 1972, the prestigious Sloan Commission on Cable Communications finally released its report on the future of broadcasting. After spending eighteen months and $500,000 of the late Alfred Sloan, Jr.'s money, the commission—made up of sixteen distinguished economists, attorneys, educators, scientists, and public figures, but no well-known TV viewers—concluded that cable television was the most promising thing to come along since commercial television. In general, the study was received with delight and some astonishment by members of the cable TV industry. They couldn't have done better if they had written it themselves.

"That's not quite true," protested a rival foundation executive. "The cable operators' own public relations men would have charged twice as much for it."

Commercial broadcasting is described in the report as the television of scarcity, and cable TV as the television of abundance. The commissioners predict that turning cable loose from all restraints, including regulation by the FCC (which hasn't been able to regulate commercial broadcasting for 30 years) and opening the door to pay TV, will encourage a diversity of entertainment, public affairs, news and opinion programs, as well as a multitude of services.

It's understandable that the cable TV industry is a little embarrassed by such high praise for its potential. The commission has a lot of faith in a group of communicators who, in the first twenty years or so of cable, have not done a noticeably impressive job of enriching the programming available to their subscribers.

"*60 Minutes*" once gave some inkling of the kinds of programs which will be available in the Golden Age of TV by reviewing the cable system in Grand Junction, Colorado. The big show out there this season is Bingo. I happen to think that's not such a bad programming idea, compared to what the networks are offering.

The stories I've read in the papers about the Sloan Commission study aren't very clear about how cable will actually bring us to the promised land. But I gather one of the great hopes for the future is a technique called "distant importation of signals."

This means a cable operator in New York can pick up a signal from a station in Philadelphia or Baltimore and bring the program to his subscribers in New York. While commercial broadcasters have always been against this practice of getting something for nothing as being basically immoral, the cable people have been saying for years that without it the industry can go nowhere. Where it will go with the freedom to import the collected works of out-of-town stations I am not quite certain. Most TV stations in the country already run the same shows.

Pay TV is another guarantee for diversity the Sloan Commission is enthusiastic about, and with good reason. It might open, say, twenty channels for movies the networks won't run. Yet what would prevent the pay TV moguls from using fifteen channels for movies like *The Love Machine* and five for pornography? Hollywood producers have traditionally taken advantage of the open marketplace to pander to the worst possible public taste. Not that there is anything wrong with nineteen channels of X-rated movies, as long as one channel is open for an occasional "Walt Disney on Parade."

Everything in the Sloan Commission report is technically possible, and I would feel better about its probability if the cable operators were men with especially strong feelings of social responsibility.

A week or so before the Sloan Commission report was published, one of the cable TV industry's leading spokesmen, after years of public service, was sentenced to five years in prison and a $10,000 fine. Irving Kahn, the former president of TelePrompter, is the kind of loud-mouthed venture capitalist who in the nineteenth century might have gone into gold mines. But in 1966, he wanted to give the people of Johnstown, Pennsylvania, the advantages of cable TV that could come with granting Tele-Prompter an exclusive franchise.

"There never was a time when I had the slightest intention of bribing Mayor [Kenneth] Tompkins and the other Johnstown officials," Kahn explained before the U.S. District Court in Manhattan in a statement that should live in the annals of broadcasting morality. He admitted making payments of $15,000 to three Johnstown officials. "The sole reason I paid them any money was to protect my company from having its business destroyed. I yielded to the pressure of these corrupt officials to keep them from harming TelePrompter, not to gain favors for the company. I strongly feel I'm not guilty of bribery."

As a member of The Committee for a Free Irving Kahn and

Against Pay TV, I am not without bias in this case. What disturbs The Committee for a Free Irving Kahn most is the harsh sentence imposed by Judge Constance Baker Motley. Kahn is the statesman of the industry. For example, his cable system in Manhattan gives subscribers not only all the regular commercial TV programs, but the Ranger and Knick games too.

A more fitting punishment for Kahn than a jail term, if he is truly guilty, would be five years of watching cable television. Or any TV. "Don't worry about Irving," explained one of his admirers, who declined to join the committee. "If he ever goes to jail, he will be very good for the prison system. He'll turn it into the greatest business in the world. All of a sudden everybody will be wanting to own license plates for every room in the house, or something. Look at the way he got TelePrompter stock up to forty times its earnings, and it's all puff. The man is a genius."

The Follies of the 70's, as outlined in the Sloan Commission report, will be followed by the Scandals of the 80's. The American people probably won't wake up to the fact that cable TV has already gone down the tube until they see the cable-originated school board meetings being interrupted every ten minutes for local commercials. Those "Buy Your Lamb Chops at Mike's Market" pitches will make Madison Avenue broadcasting seem like the Golden Age of TV.

Smith, Howard K. McLuhan said television has
made print obsolete. In one area of the medium print seems to be making a comeback. While the rest of TV is blowing its mind with psychedelic music, with-it plots and McLuhanistic projects for the future, ABC has been slowly increasing the amount of print it puts on the screen whenever Howard K. Smith makes one of his commentaries on its seven o'clock news show.

The anti-McLuhan trend started with the one word COMMENTARY. Sometime after another authority on the medium

(Vice President Agnew) attacked TV news for bias, the word COMMENTARY began appearing in triplicate. A few days ago, Howard K. Smith's distinguished portrait came on the screen with another bit of print superimposed: his autograph.

What the network is trying to do is let us know that the sixty-second essay Smith delivers at the end of his show three or four times a week is his own opinion. They have stopped short of flashing the noted commentator's driver's license and fingerprints on the screen.

Smoking on TV. Once on an educational television

show called "Newsfront," I heard Jerry Rubin, the noted revolutionary, announce that he was about to turn on. He did not ask the host, Mitchell Krauss, if it was all right to smoke. He just lit a match to the necessary and said, "I'm stoned out of my mind." A cheap thrill ran down my spine. I was experiencing a new high in educational television entertainment.

As I watched him smoke the joint, I began to grow alarmed. Nothing wonderful was happening to him. For the thirty minutes or so that Rubin was presumably under the influence of pot, he remained the same rude, belligerent, immature, incoherent person the now generation has come to adore. He was no advertisement for smoking marijuana; one of the sales points for grass is that it makes you a beautiful person.

Many viewers at home, it turned out, believed Jerry Rubin. They called police stations all over New York City to report the incident. At Channel 13, one of the sixteen educational stations in the East which carried "Newsfront," the switchboard lit up with phone calls from the precincts. "I understand you are having a pot party on the air," one police captain said to the Channel 13 telephone operator.

Something the police don't know about the behind-the-scenes affairs of educational television is that the switchboard operator always keeps the TV set in the reception room tuned to commercial stations. Thus it was necessary for the woman to leave the phones and change channels to verify the claims of an orgy on Channel 13.

Snipping and Cutting.

There are many mysteries connected with the showing of old movies on TV. I've never been able to figure out, for example, why a 90-minute movie takes 2½ hours to show on TV—and must be cut anyway. My nominee for the worst crime ever perpetrated against our movie inheritance occurred in 1970 when Channel 5 (WNEW-TV) cut the "Win One for the Gipper" scene from "Knute Rockne."

Sponsors.

The Mobil Oil Corporation announced a while ago that it was giving a grant of $1,200,000 to the Corporation for Public Broadcasting to renew its funding of Masterpiece Theater—a Public Television show which re-runs BBC hits—until June 1973. The news upset one of Mobil's stockholders.

"They are wasting the corporation's assets by sponsoring Public Broadcasting's programs," the outraged stockholder told me. "We'd be better off buying time on the NBC or ABC football games." The New York investor said he was planning to institute a minority stockholder's suit against Mobil, based on the legal principle of *ultra vires* (i.e., a corporation has exceeded the bounds of its charter by not engaging in activities it is chartered to do). "We are not into television," he explained. "At least, I haven't noticed that we've changed our name to Mobil Public Television & Oil Corp."

The fellow is obviously a radical. But I tried to reason with

138

him anyway by pointing out what a good charitable thing Mobil was doing by underwriting Public Television shows. "Charity is not one of the responsibilities of our corporation," he explained. "Particularly an inefficient charity. I wouldn't mind if we were helping an efficient charity, like the March of Dimes. But Public Television is an inefficient charity."

He cited an article in TV Guide about public television, titled "Is Anybody Watching?" The gist of the article is that Public TV's ratings are low. This is news in some places. "The really surprising thing," I tried to reassure the stockholder, "is not that Public Television has so few viewers, but so many."

"The argument for advertising on the network's pro football games," he explained, "is that people will buy more Mobil Oil. All we're doing by advertising on the Masterpiece Theater is creating a wish to go to England to see British television. Is that what we want to do—promote BBC products? We don't even sell Mobil in England. If the name of our company was BP, that would be something else."

The stockholder didn't seem to realize why Mobil Oil got into the business of sponsoring Public Broadcasting shows in the first place. So I tried to explain how it had happened.

A couple of years ago, according to a usually reliably informed source, a problem came up at a secret meeting of the Public Television establishment. "Who will buy BBC re-runs for Public TV?" somebody asked. "It has to be some corporation with a bad reputation for polluting the air," a Public TV consultant answered immediately. The Mobil Oil people were approached through intermediaries. "Your company has been accused of polluting the air," Mobil's top executives were told. "You have to do something to offset the bad reputation. What would you like your name to be associated with instead of pollution?"

Without blinking an eye, Mobil said, "Highclass British drama!" "And it worked!" I told the stockholder. "What do you associate Mobil with today—pollution or English drama?"

"Pollution," he said.

"Where would the Corporation for Public Broadcasting get the money to continue underwriting the Masterpiece Theater if your suit wins?" I asked.

"Let Xerox do it," he explained. "They want to be good guys." Instead of sponsoring public broadcasting shows, the stockholder said, the corporation should be trying to pollute more beaches. "If they keep polluting the beaches," he explained, "there won't be any more beaches left to pollute. Then all those maniacs would stop complaining about it in the press. And we can get out of public television."

"The Star-Spangled Banner." Robert

Meyner, in his second New Jersey gubernatorial race in 1957, bought time for an election eve talkathon back-to-back with Malcolm Forbes, his Republican opponent. Meyner went on the air first, in prime time. About five minutes before Forbes' show was scheduled to begin, Meyner's campaign manager, Robert J. Burkhardt, ordered the playing of "The Star-Spangled Banner." Then the video went dark and the audio silent. When Forbes finally came on the air, the TV audience had diminished considerably. That's what I call really using the medium.

140

Superdog. Lassie's problems seem to date back to his show of January 4, 1970. That night a child ran into the street after a ball. Smelling impending danger, the superstar raced into the street after her. Lassie nudged the girl out of the path of a runaway car in the nick of time. The girl's life was saved, but Lassie was hit by the car.

Suddenly Lassie acted strangely. He didn't seem to remember who he was. "Amnesia," the script writers told us.

On the show of January 11, Lassie was still wandering the streets of San Francisco in a fog. "Lassie, you've got to remember who you are," soliloquized his master, the forest ranger, leading the search for the missing superdog in another part of the city.

By January 18 Lassie was drifting around the city like a hippie, sleeping in parks, living off the land and running away from the police. "How long can you keep this search up?" asked the ranger's friend on January 25. "Until we find Lassie," the ranger said, his jaw tightening. "I've taken a leave of absence until we do."

Finally, in the last minutes of the fourth installment in the incredible saga of a dog's search for his true identity, Lassie miraculously found what he was looking for: his mind and his past. It wasn't clear to me what brought the great dog back to his senses. Nor did I care at the time. It was enough that Lassie no longer suffered from the dreaded scourge of dogkind, amnesia.

Those are the dry facts of the case. The last few weeks I've

been able to think about the larger questions raised by Lassie's affliction. First, how did he know that he had amnesia?

The director of the ASPCA in New York said he had never heard of a dog having amnesia. "This is a neurological problem," he advised. "You should consult a specialist."

Still, my theory is that Lassie, during the period of January 4–25, was suffering from a case of hysterical amnesia. Psychologically, he was trying to run away from the show, then in its sixteenth consecutive year. Traditionally collies are high strung dogs (the male of the species less so than females, the reason Lassie is always played by a male). Add to this the pressure of ratings, the early casting calls, and associating with the type people in the television business. Lassie was trying to drop out of Hollywood society which not even a dog can stand. Lassie was having a free floating experience in the streets of San Francisco for a month, a relief from his responsibilities and chores. What disturbs me is that children identify with Lassie. We have enough trouble these days without a dog show preaching copping out.

Talk Show Hosts. The secret of a talk show's success is the predictability of the host. Viewers feel comfortable

knowing exactly what will happen in ninety minutes night after night. This may explain why it is common practice for the same guests to make the rounds of the shows, like nightwatchmen clocking in, to discuss the same things. Surprises throw the host off key, something that isn't taken lightly.

Every host has a key word which is a clue to his discomfort. When Jack Parr said *pal*, as in "Now listen, pal," insiders always knew the guest was making his farewell appearance. The most frequently heard clue on the air today is "You're great. We'll see you again soon." That means "get rid of him."

Robert King, an actor who has appeared on some fifty talk shows in the last few years, has done for talk shows what Dewey did for libraries. He has figured out a way to classify them. The system he uses is based on the manner in which each host reacts to a five-word sentence: "I am going to a concert."

If said to Johnny Carson, King claims the host of "The Tonight Show" would answer: "Oh, is that what they call it nowadays!"

Mike Douglas, according to King, would react this way: "Bob, do you want to tell the folks about the concert?"

Donald O'Connor would respond, "You are going to a concert? Our next guest . . ."

"That's very interesting," Merv Griffin would offer. "Is that the concert at Carnegie Hall or Lincoln Center where Isaac Stern is playing the violin or piano?"

David Frost would say, "That's marvelous. Just magnificent. Do you enjoy concerts?" One has the feeling Frost is very interested.

The sentence would remind Joey Bishop that his cameraman's wife just had a baby.

Dave Garroway would say nothing.

"This Is Your Government." By dabbling in public service, the commercial networks are diluting

the function of noncommercial television. The networks should devote themselves to "private service." Public service should be the business of public broadcasting. The way it is now, the Corporation for Public Broadcasting is up to its neck in providing entertainment, a lot of which is better than what the commercial networks are producing.

When the president wants to give one of his political science lectures on government, why should he have to worry about what show he is preempting and how many votes he may be losing? CPB, with its tax-supported facilities, could make available an hour or so to the president *every* day. If he was too busy to get to the studio to tape his show, which might be called something like "This Is Your Government," others in the administration have proven talents. CPB could also make equal time available to the administration's critics for a show called "This Is Your Next Government."

Thursday Night at the Movies. See "Monday Night at the Movies."

Troy, ancient. See "Bacchus."

Tuesday Night at the Movies. See "Monday Night at the Movies."

TV Campaigning. On balance, 1970 was a black year for television in politics. TV candidates Richard Ottinger

of New York and Howard Metzenbaum of Ohio—two of the medium's finest products—lost. So did dozens of other candidates who spent millions on commercials.

The only consistent winners on November 3 were the broadcasters. Like bookmakers, they collect the vigorish regardless of who wins the race. Maybe all the talk about television's ability to build a false image is only a ploy by the TV station owners and the advertising agencies to get politicians to spend their money on TV instead of squandering it on newspapers, billboards and direct payments to voters. The five leading image-makers— David Garth, Charles Guggenheim, Roger Ailes, Joseph Napolitan, Harry Treleavan—had thirteen winners, thirteen losers and one still unresolved.

That so many people fear the influence TV may have had on the elections comes as no surprise to me. In the early days of the medium, TV was always being described as a threat to one art form or another. Who will ever forget that it was supposed to kill the movies?

The TV Candidate. Some critics blame the defeat of certain candidates on television when the real reason they lost is that they didn't get enough votes. They keep saying there is something unfair about using television to get elected. Perhaps the fairest way to cope with the electronic age in politics is to require the candidates who use it to follow television's other rules as well. For instance, a TV candidate's election might be canceled after thirteen weeks if the sponsor (the people) didn't approve of his performance in office.

TV Editorials. The five or six minutes a day local TV stations have been turning over to editorializing since WCBS-

TV began it all in the New York area in 1960, are very important to the broadcasters. It gives them the chance to speak out on the issues, such as man-eating sharks. The stations are usually against them. ("Only one man has been killed in four years," a typical editorial on this problem tends to run. "But that's one too many.")

Christmas seals, drug abuse, littering and careless driving are other subjects which have felt the lash of broadcasters' tongues. My favorite is still the WCBS-TV editorial which came out in support of *The Saturday Evening Post.*

Not back in 1966, when the *Post* could have used the editorial support in its fight against Madison Avenue, but on December 12, 1970. *The Saturday Evening Post* died in 1969.

UHF. Frankly, the promise of cable television hasn't excited me as much as it has most people. I am still waiting for UHF to fulfill its great promises.

It was only a few seasons back that the FCC, the UHF station owners and the critics were saying that the extra dial of stations with those big numbers would open up the door to program diversity, missing on the VHF dial. What they didn't tell us was that in order to tune in those great programs on UHF you had to have the fingers of a safecracker.

UHF stations, far from bringing us into the Golden Age of TV, are in financial trouble all over the country. Not enough people are watching the stations to attract advertisers. This is a minor problem, which easily could be corrected by the FCC's passing a rule requiring all pro-football games to be carried on UHF stations.

Used Car Monuments. There are now 20,000

abandoned cars strewn about the American landscape, Sander Vanocur, the anchorman on "First Tuesday," observed in April, 1970. This year Americans will abandon 2,500 automobiles every day, enough to fill six acres of ground. As a public service, I suggest the establishment of an organization like the Ford Foundation which will underwrite experiments in solving the problem of what to do with old cars. The Used Car Foundation might begin saving the countryside by urging the National Park Service to make Industrial Revolution Landmarks out of the remaining automobile junkyards.

Not everybody thinks the junkyards are eyesores. They are little bits of Americana, something many of us have grown up with and want to preserve in a natural state so that our children can have them, too. A good junkyard makes one think about the meaning of life and death in an industrial society, the hopes and ambitions of upwardly mobile people, the money that went into financing all those dream cars that TV made us want.

At the same time, a Used Car Foundation would tackle the problem of developing a truly disposable car. A new car today lasts about five years. Advanced technology can make it possible for a car to last even less time by making more parts out of miracle plastic and cardboard.

When you buy a new car you would be required to fold up

the old one and put it in the trunk of the new car. This would automatically cut the number of automobiles in half. It is the ultimate in planned obsolescence, something called *planned disappearance.*

The cardboard car would be just as safe as the metal car. Furthermore, police could make you tear up your car for serious traffic violations. But it is a long way off.

The most practical solution to car disposal today is to stop pressing old cars into three-foot cubes of junk. There is no mechanical reason why they can't be pressed into one-by-five rectangles, which would fit into trunks of cars equipped with heavy-duty springs. Everybody has junk in their trunks anyway, and a little more won't matter.

Used Conspiracies. The premise of *The News Twisters,* a recently published book by Edith Efron, the prominent *TV Guide* writer, is that the news departments of the three networks represent the most powerful communications tool in the history of man. After the presidential nominating conventions in 1968, word filtered down from the highest councils of the networks that NBC, CBS and ABC had decided to join together and elect the Democratic candidate. In some way, the *TV Guide* writer heard about the conspiracy.

Miss Efron set about to carefully document the networks' coverage that year. She compiled an audio-tape record of all the network news shows, and spent years analyzing their editorial content. These words were pro-Democratic candidate, these words were anti-Republican candidate and so forth. According to her evidence, there really must have been a conspiracy.

Actually, there is nothing new in Miss Efron's thesis. Conservative writers like Roscoe Drummond have written of it before. Vice President Agnew has mentioned it, too.

What surprises me after reading the book is the election results in 1968. As everyone knows, Hubert Humphrey ran against what's-his-name in that election. Anybody, the experts were saying in 1968, could beat this fellow. Despite the conspiracy and the combined weight of the three networks' news departments' best manipulators, the sure loser won.

Miss Efron's conclusion is that the networks terribly abused their awesome power and something ought to be done to curb them. The fact is that if you accept the premise of *The News Twisters* you can be led to an even more startling conclusion. The networks can't even fix an election. When they spend two or three years planning each season's entertainment programs the best they can do is produce eight out of ten shows that fail. How could any group that gave us "The Jimmy Stewart Show" successfully steal an election? Why, they couldn't even rig a quiz show successfully. The only thing television executives have really succeeded at is holding onto their jobs year after year.

Would you buy a used conspiracy from those people?

Even though this may horrify Edith Efron, I look forward to the day when the networks actually know how to do what she accused them of doing in 1968. She says it's not in the public interest. I say ineptitude is never in the public interest. Once the networks understand the public enough to influence them at the polls, maybe they'll understand the public enough to stimulate, educate and entertain them.

Values. "In terms of its values," Paul Krassner observes, "television is schizophrenic. One hour you see a documentary decrying the disappearance of a species, the next hour you see a game show, like "The Price Is Right," where the prize is a fur coat made from the disappearing species."

Vietnam. The most memorable event in the history of the television documentary occurred the night of December 21, 1971 when an NBC narrator told the TV audience that his network's news department had been wrong in one of its judgments. The story NBC said it blew was the Vietnam war—since 1961.

In the first minute of the first hour of a two-hour, two-night study titled "An NBC White Paper: Vietnam Hindsight," newsman Floyd Kalber confessed: "To the degree that we in the media paid any attention at all to that small dirty war in those years, we almost wholly reported the position of the government. We had no more foresight about what the war would become than the men in Washington who made the decisions. We did not foresee and we did not understand."

What could have driven writer and producer Fred Freed to

shatter an ancient tradition in so uncouth a manner in the opening minute of "Vietnam Hindsight"? Maybe it was a secret belief that the TV documentary hasn't long to live, so he might just as well start breaking up the old institution right then. In any event, until that night I had been spared the shock of seeing a network confess to error, though I'd often suspected they weren't perfect.

The remainder of Part I presented a unique kind of defense for TV journalism. Kalber seemed to be asking us, "If distinguished men like Walt Rostow and Roswell Gilpatric were wrong about Vietnam, with all the best intelligence money could buy, how could a mere TV network news department be expected to have any independent judgments? Are we not all equally guilty?"

Kalber and Freed reminded me of the men who go to a synagogue on the Day of Atonement and say, "I have sinned. But Sam sinned, Jack sinned, Bill sinned, Melvin sinned, Mark sinned, George sinned, Jonathan sinned, Sid sinned, Stan sinned . . ."

In that first minute of "Vietnam Hindsight" there was an air of soul-searching more common to a purge trial than a TV documentary. It might have been useful for the TV viewer if Kalber and Freed had continued in the mood of recantation and remorse by naming a few names at their network who had been bilked by the government.

This distinguished list would have started with former NBC President Robert Kintner, under whose hawk-eyed view the network's newsmen started disappearing into the government's pocket. It also would have included Freed himself, whose landmark documentary, "American White Paper: U.S. Foreign Policy" (September 7, 1965), was the first foreign policy show to occupy a full evening of prime time (7:30–11:00 P.M.) and was the network's definitive statement on the war for the next six years. Bringing up the rear on the list would have been fieldhands like Kalber who did the actual reporting of the war. Of course, any network newsman could argue that he didn't know what he was doing while he was covering Vietnam because he

151

was under the influence of money; in that drugged state, TV
newsmen have been known to do or say anything that was popular
with their bosses.

To have been most constructive, "Vietnam Hindsight" could
have gone into the limitations of TV journalism. What viewers
have never been told is that television newsmen are not out to
get the truth, but to get on the air. Their fees are based on air
time. Vietnam was a place where a TV newsman could make a
name and a bundle for himself.

The easiest way for the fieldhands in the Far East to move up
was to be caught in "a shoot-'em-up," a fire-fight. The competition
was always keen. The network brass sent over three or four young
reporters. One man went three miles into the bush, the next went
five. This led as often to death as to an understanding of what
was really going on. A famous cable in the archives of network
journalism (CBS News branch) reads: "NBC JUST HAD X [a
well-known correspondent] WOUNDED. WHY NOT US?"

Violence and Children. I had been meaning
to say a few words congratulating NBC on the good news that it

152

was planning to spend $500,000 for a five-year study on the impact of TV violence on children. It sounded like a gesture in the spirit of Alfred Nobel, who took the money he made by inventing dynamite and underwrote a number of prizes, including one for the individual who has done the most to encourage world peace.

Then I read that all the networks are funding studies on the same subject. It was all very confusing until I learned that the National Institute of Mental Health has a study coming out on the impact of television on children's behavior.

The atmosphere in televisionland today must be very much like it was in Winston-Salem shortly before the surgeon-general's report on the relationship between smoking and cancer was published in 1964. The tobacco companies didn't know what the surgeon-general was going to say, but they knew it wouldn't be anything good.

Violence and Realism. What I miss most on
TV is "meaningless violence." Remember the old bar room brawls, now extinct? A woman suffragette group would walk into a saloon in a western and try to talk politics. For no good reason, everybody would push on the poker tables at once and the fight would be on. The meaningful fights we have today last 20 seconds, mere scuffles. But the great meaningless fights of yesteryear lasted five minutes. They were a kind of ballet as carefully staged as professional wrestling. In the history of this ritual, nobody ever got hurt.

Everybody knows those brawls were supposed to be funny. The mistake television made was not showing the aftermath of violence. When you hit somebody, something happens. You break your hand. Directors should have done the next scene in a hospital room.

Directors are against this kind of realism because it theoretically slows down the plot. However, a private eye could go about his business the day after he throws a punch with his hand in a sling. The secret of his success on television is usually his keen mind anyway. The glamor of the private eye's way of life could be underscored by the purple mouse under his eye and the bruises on his face.

That at least would make a statement about violence. The trouble is TV can't put a rule like that on paper. If they said, "When a guy gets hit over the head he has to have a headache afterward," the producers would say, "You mean I can show the gash on the head with the blood streaming down . . .?" They're always looking for loopholes.

The Weatherman Technique. Everybody knows how the television ratings work. In the Nielsen's 1,200 families are used to tell us what 200,000,000 Americans are watching. If one of those Nielsen families went to visit their relatives on a specific night, the noted statistician Art Buchwald once explained, that meant 150,000 families went to visit their relatives that same night.

Commercial networks need ratings because there is no other way to distinguish programs.

The dignity of public television requires the use of more

sophisticated polling techniques than the Nielsen. The Weather-man Technique—named after the first forecaster who predicted the weather by calling home and asking, "Ma, how does your back feel?"—consists of questioning one typical viewer in depth. "Pop," the interviewer asked the random sampling, "did you see our great special on ecology?" "Only three guys in the bar were watching it," the respondent reports, "the others had the football game on."

"We could make out very well in the ratings," explained one public television executive who was pushing for weighted ratings, "if a typical viewer like Marya Mannes was worth, say, fifteen times as much as one telephone operator. This is not to downgrade the telephone business as a glamor profession. Those girls get to talk to people all over the world."

What public TV should be interested in is how many people of influence watch their programs. If only twenty people are watching an ecology show, and they happen to be presidents of chemical companies polluting the environment, that carries more weight than a network show which has 20,000,000 viewers, half of whom are under nine.

Probably the most effective way to measure public television's impact would be to limit the survey of who's watching to people who have a vested interest in it, say, the top executives of the public broadcasting establishment.

Wednesday Night at the Movies.
See "Monday Night at the Movies."

Wiretapping as Entertainment. The
poor image wiretapping has in American society today may be caused by television's failure to do anything to popularize eaves-

dropping with the masses. In the seven years the ABC series "The FBI" has been on the air, for example, Efrem Zimbalist, Jr. has never had a program hailing the exploits of the bureau's wire-tappers. They are the best in the world, according to authorities, if you don't count the Russian, Chinese, Albanian and Cuban secret police.

There are many interesting taps in the FBI files which deserve public exposure. Victor Navasky—who spent six years studying the working of the Justice Department and the FBI for his brilliant bestseller *Kennedy Justice*—believes there is enough material in the FBI files for a spin-off of the Zimbalist show to be called "Can You Tap This?"

As Navasky sees it, there would be a panel of expert eaves-droppers, each a former attorney general, men of the stature of Ramsey Clark, Nick Katzenbach, William Rogers, Herb Brownell or even Tom Clark. The show would open with each regular panelist telling the story of how he, as attorney general, con-trolled J. Edgar Hoover. A laugh meter would measure who had been the most effective head of the Justice Department.

The panelist with the highest rating would be invited to spin his favorite wiretap of some government official's phone conver-sation. Then the MC would cry enthusiastically, "Can you tap this?"

In the audience participation part of the show, former FBI agents would be invited to send in bugs of conversations of private citizens, which they had taken with them when leaving the bureau. The panelists would rate the taps on such criteria as most threating to national security, dirtiest, most libelous and slanderous, containing the most raw, unevaluated data some of which may be true, and so forth.

Women in TV. I once wanted to interview a woman in programming at any of the three major networks.

Any woman; I wasn't particular. The only criterion was that she had to have something important to do with developing, buying or planning the programs for the new season.

There was nobody to talk to.

I don't mean to imply there are no women in important jobs at the networks today. ABC, for example, has a woman vice-president. But she's in personnel.

What is odd about this situation is that among those viewers who take TV seriously (five to six hours a day of studying the medium), women are certainly prominent. They especially know more than anybody about daytime television.

It is fashionable to sneer at what the networks put on the air during the daytime hours. But it is this drudge of the business that pays for the great experiments on nighttime television. Wouldn't it be a good idea for a network to have an authority on what women really like to see involved in making these decisions?

Wooden Panels. The TV discussion show—the
most effective instrument for keeping viewers informed that the medium has thought of since it was invented in 1927—was best defined by Brian Sharoff. A New York state assemblyman and host of an obscure discussion series loved by the literally dozens of people who watch New York's WNYC-TV, Sharoff explained: "We put five people together and see what happens when wood rubs against wood."

World (flat). See "A Balanced Documentary."

World (round). See "A Balanced Documentary."

Z-Rays.

Less is known about Z-rays than about gamma rays (see "Gamma Rays"). But everybody who has ever had a TV repairman in his house knows how they work.

Sets repaired at home always work perfectly while the repairman is on the premises, even though he may have removed your set's best components to sell to another customer. That is because the repairman may exude Z-rays, a type of electromagnetic waves picked up from working in close contact with TV sets for years.

Conversely, the TV set stops working perfectly as soon as the TV repairman leaves. This may be caused by the absence of Z-rays.

After TV: What?

I've written many serious things about TV in the last few years. Sometimes these terrific suggestions about improving the medium have been phrased in a light manner. Just because it may sound funny doesn't mean I am not serious. On the other hand, I've written things that were meant to be funny which people have taken seriously. TV situation-comedy writers have the same problem.

For five years I have been turning over the honorariums from my writings about TV to a nonprofit organization, the Marvin Kitman Fund. Like Ford, Carnegie, and Sloan, Kitman has underwritten a study on the future of television. To honor the fifth anniversary of its founder's involvement with the medium, the Fund published in 1972 its landmark study, titled "After TV: What?", excerpts of which follow.

1. The Problem: A recent survey asked viewers in New York, "What's your favorite TV program?" Seven out of ten respondents couldn't name one.

The second question, asked only of those who had a favorite program, was tougher: "Which network is it on?" A majority of the respondents' eyes went blank, then glazed over. Many had no opinion. Others thought the network was "somewhere between

2 and 7" (channel numbers in the New York area). A few got the answer partially right, guessing one out of the three letters, usually the last "C," as in NBC and ABC. A high percentage of viewers, the survey discovered, confused these two networks because of the similarity of their initials (CBS was rarely mentioned by anybody, even erroneously).

2. The Conclusions: This is a disturbing situation. The commercial networks spend millions of dollars every year to establish their separate identities by creating new programs, promoting them on the air, advertising heavily in newspapers and *TV Guide.* Yet the public is so ungrateful that it won't even take the trouble to keep the networks straight. Obviously, it's a case of throwing away good stockholders' money after bad.

On the other hand, it may be that there are simply too many commercial networks. During the first 25 years of television, the industry gave the American people the best entertainment and enlightenment (news and public affairs) that the best minds money can buy were able to think of. Now, however, the networks are just repeating themselves each September. Competition, the Fund found, has reached a dead end in the medium; it seems there is not enough creative talent around to support three independent networks. If the three could be merged in some way, the result would be the greatest little commerical broadcasting operation in the world.

3. Recommendations: The Nixon Administration indicated a desire to break up the present broadcasting system by initiating its silly anti-trust suit (in 1972). The Fund, too, believes the structure of television should be reshaped in a rational, orderly manner. Moreover, it feels that TV will never change unless all the existing licenses are recalled. Congress has the power to do this by passing a new law. Therefore we propose the adoption of a bill to be called the Broadcasting Act of 1984. The date was selected not only because it marks the 50th anniversary of the Broadcasting Act of 1934, responsible for the current rules of the game, but in anticipation that the legislation will require lengthy hearings.

As guardians of the public's interest in the airwaves, Congress should explain to the license holders: "Look, we didn't know what we were doing in 1934 when we began giving away the licenses. But now we've learned from experience. Let's start all over again." In gratitude to all the entrepreneurs who risked thousands to make millions in the old days—when few knew that a TV license was as good as a permit to print money—the lawmakers could take steps to assure that nobody would suffer undue economic deprivation. For example, they might proclaim a five-year moratorium allowing all licensed stations to make as much profit as possible (for most licensees, this would not necessitate any substantial change in practice) so that every millionaire broadcaster would be able to retire as a multi-millionaire.

The new TV licenses should be distributed in the following manner: Every city that previously had three commercial network affiliates would henceforth have one. To be known as the Conglomerate American Network (combining the first initials of the three merged corporations in tribute to all they have done for television in the past), this new entity would be required by law to carry all the entertainment programs the people love (the so-called "escapist junk").

Because of the economic inefficiency of the present system, no network can afford to produce more than 13 or 14 new shows in a popular Western series like *Bonanza*. The new conglomerate, however, could run 13 weeks each of *Bonanza, Gunsmoke, Alias Smith and Jones,* etc. Consequently, there would be no need to schedule reruns, unless viewers asked for them by writing letters to their congressmen.

To protect the people's free and total access to their escapist junk without interruption from the world of reality, the new CAN network should be prohibited from carrying any public service programming (news or public affairs), and from being preempted by Presidential speeches or press conferences. All the boring stuff should be left to public TV.

Stockholders in the three existing networks would be issued shares in the new conglomerate. All Madison Avenue agency money would go into the merged outlet, since it would be the only wheel in town. The profit picture for investors should be even brighter than in the old days.

The new station franchises should be open to all comers. Previous licensees would be judged by their past records in broadcasting. This might force most of the old people out of business, leaving the industry to the handful who have never looked at TV regularly: the Paleys, Goldensons and Sarnoffs. A special rule could be made to bar these special cases.

At the same time, no one need be fired from the staffs of the present three networks, for each top job in the conglomerate could be filled by three men. Given that most of the key executives have worked at all the networks, they should not have any loyalty problems. Though initially the committees would be larger than in the existing system, over the months one man will naturally emerge at the top. The others, with corporate knives in their backs, will discover that their true talent lies in hotel management or owning a McDonald's franchise.

If competition used to be so important in commercial television, where it is needed today is in public TV. Accordingly, the Broadcasting Act of 1984 should require that there be two public networks, one pro-government and other anti-government. To accomplish this, one of the two eliminated commercial outlets in each city should be incorporated into a "peoples network," open to all dissident groups (from Democrats to Gay Liberationists) who want to change the existing order. In most areas we already have stations run by the Corporation for Public Broadcasting arm of the government. These old public channels will continue to carry State-of-the-Union messages, Presidential press conferences and other such propaganda. (Of course, the way the government has used the commercial networks the last 10 years, you really couldn't tell whether General William C. Westmoreland or the late General David Sarnoff was in charge anyway.)

That still leaves open one station in each city. Under the new act this channel would be given directly to the advertising agencies. They could then run an all-commercial network, with an occasional spot announcement, like "We interrupt this Alka-Seltzer program for a brief message from our newsroom" (if they were able to find anybody willing to pay for it). Eventually the ad men, who have their fingers on the pulse of what the public wants, might even try to sell space in their commercials for an old movie, a live Broadway play or a soap opera.

Finally, if the Broadcasting Act of 1984—which the Kitman Fund believes to be the best hope for diversity in television—does not succeed, we can try something else another half-century later.

A Note on Source Materials. All the factual errors in this book are attributable to information supplied by my usually reliably informed sources. For example, the San Diego Plan, described on Page 128, actually took place in Palm Springs, California. It's such errors as these that lead to either libel suits or Pulitzer Prizes. Richard Harding Davis and Louella Parsons would both be proud of my work as a journalist.

Marie Torre of the *New York Herald Tribune* went to jail rather than reveal her sources. (That was the landmark case in which the noted TV critic—now the hostess of an early-morning TV talk show in Pittsburgh—refused to tell the court who at CBS told her that Judy Garland was fat, a major issue in the television of the 1950s.) But I am not ashamed of my sources. If it was a crime to have stolen their ideas and jokes—as some may have concluded by reading this far into the book—it was only petty larceny. The ideas and jokes were the best my sources were capable of. Space limitations in the text of the book prevented giving credit where credit is due.

Before I name names, I would like to point out there are two kinds of sources reporters use: unimpeachable sources and impeachable sources. These are not fixed. An "unimpeachable source," when he gives you a story that doesn't stand the test of truth, is severely rebuked and demoted to an "impeachable source."

My leading impeachable sources in these pages were men like Gen. David Sarnoff, Wiliam Paley, Leonard Goldenson, Julian Goodman, Frank Stanton, and Elton Rule.

My unimpeachable sources (in the order their contributions appear) are: Neil Postman, Bill Kraslovsky, Al Slep, Gene Shalit, John Wicklein, Reuven Frank, Al Levin, Angela Solomon, Gene Walsh, Marty Solow, Joe Dine, Tony Geiss, Stan Isaacs, Art Alpert, Dave Schmerler, Richard Lingeman, Victor Navasky, Diane Soorikian, Mari Yanofsky, Harvey Jacobs, Mark Schubin, Calvin Trillin, Joyce Teitz, Lou Klein, John Chancellor, Wally Westfeldt, Tony Randall, Dave Roland, Stuart Sucherman, Bud Rukeyser, Larry Schilling, Charles Weingarten, Jonathan Cerf, Christopher Cerf, Steve Strassberg, Howard Hughes, Pat Throne, Herb Wurth, Hermy Traviesis, John Horn, Bill Greeley, Eric Lasher, Shad Northshield, Billy Blank, Paul Klein, Rita Solow, Larry Schneider, Sid Bakal, Jerry Toobin, Don Kaplan, Jim Day, Gwen Davis, Hughes Rudd, Jim Butler, Dick Wald, John Crosby, Alan Levine, Roger Ailes, Arlene Handel, Mort Gerberg, Jim Byrnes, Nick Johnson, Jim Bouton, Len Shecter, Peter Nord, Alan Alda, Joe Derby, Noel Parmental, Dick Ballinger, Sid Zion, Brian Sharoff, Mark Grunes, Tony Shaw, Les Brown, Alan Abel, Frank Oski, Donny Blank, Ira Glasser, Tom Mackin, George Salvatore, Joel Blank, Edith Ialeggio, Ed Ritchie, Dick Schaap, Bob Shanks, Wilfrid Sheed, Beano Cook, Dennis Wholey, Arnold Auerbach, Garry Belkin, Art Buchwald, Judith Gerberg, Peter Edmiston, Fred Feretti, Dan Greenberg, Bob Hatch, Bart Jones, Ben Kubasik, Jeff Lyons, Milton Hoffman, Joe Muzio, Susan Edmiston, Nora Ephron, Lou Schwartz, Sylvia Davis, Mitch Krause, Mike Levine, Bettye Spinner, Vic Ghedalia, David Webster, Len Chaimowitz, Woody Allen, Mervin Block, David Frost, Jerry DellaFemia, Marty Puris, Bob Fresco,

165

Marvin Honig, Marc Levitt, Steve Scneuer, Joe Koenenn, Judy Santarsiero, Merv Griffin, Dea Theodore F. Peterson, Neil Hickey, Sandy Ripley, Robert Ludlum, Roger Youman, Carl Ally, Russell Baker, Bob Kotlowitz, Dan Enright, Eileen Argue.

And last, but not least, Sam Glick of Radio City who holds the broadcasting record for the fastest time in running to the press with a story.

Finally, for the sources whose names are misspelled and to those whose names have been omitted because I have a mind like a steel sieve, my apologies. You know who you are.